MORE TALKS
FOR ALL-AGE WORSHIP

SUSAN SAYERS

First published in 1999 by
KEVIN MAYHEW LTD
Buxhall
Stowmarket
Suffolk IP14 3BW

© 1999 Kevin Mayhew Ltd

ISBN 1 84003 410 6
Catalogue No 1500301

0 1 2 3 4 5 6 7 8 9

Cover illustration: *Family of five* by Diana Ong
Reproduced by courtesy of SuperStock, London
Cover design by Jaquetta Sergeant
Edited by Peter Dainty
Typesetting by Louise Selfe
Printed and bound in Great Britain

Contents

Foreword

Following the positive reception given to *100 Talks for All-age Worship*, this second volume provides a further collection of ideas and outlines for all-age talks, with both a thematic and a biblical reference index to help the leader find material appropriate for their congregation and their service.

It is common practice in modern churches for the whole church family, from the youngest to the oldest, to come together for at least part of morning worship. This may be for a few minutes at the beginning or ending of the service, but there will also be times when the whole of worship is shared by all ages. One of the most challenging and potentially exciting aspects of such worship is the opportunity it provides for the proclamation of the Gospel and the presentation of Christian teaching in stimulating and refreshing ways.

Anyone who has had the privilege of leading all-age worship will be aware not only of its difficulties, but also of its delights – one of which is the strong sense of *sharing* which is sometimes missing from more formal worship patterns. For one thing, there is a shared understanding of the teaching. The Gospel is for all, and can be understood by all when it is expressed in terms of everyday experiences to which everyone can relate at their own level. Jesus himself knew this, and that is one of the reasons why he taught in parables. The ideas in this book aim to present the Gospel message in a way that will mean something to every member of the congregation. The shared understanding which results will have an untold spiritual impact on the corporate life of the church.

Another delight of all-age worship springs from shared participation in the teaching. Movement, speech and action are encouraged; in fact they are essential if the congregation is to feel involved, not only superficially but at a deeper level. Humour will play an important part, but more important will be the greater sense of togetherness and mutual awareness which a more open and uninhibited expression of faith and feeling make possible.

The ideas presented here are only suggestions, of course, and it is to be hoped that they will be adapted to suit the needs of particular churches, or that they will inspire other ideas which will present the Christian message in ways that are both memorable and meaningful. Expect the unexpected – the Holy Spirit can speak to us not only through the carefully prepared words of the minister or leader, but also through the uninhibited comments and actions of children and adults alike, who are learning together what God has to say to his people.

SUSAN SAYERS

THE LORD OUR GOD

God rules – O.K.?

Unless the size of your congregation makes it far too expensive, give everyone a penny. Invite everyone to look at their coin. On one side there is a picture of someone's head. Whose head is it? It belongs to Queen Elizabeth II. She is there, just as Caesar's picture was on the coin Jesus looked at (see Matthew 22:15-22), because she is the Head of State and we are her subjects. In our country there are taxes to pay to make sure that everyone, both rich and poor, can have schools, roads and hospitals. There are laws to keep, so that we can all live safely and peacefully, and there are police to check that we keep the laws. Those who break them are sent to prison or charged a fine.

Each country works out its own way of organising all this, and some are fairer than others. Each country has leaders – people who are in charge – and the country Jesus lived in was ruled by the Romans.

Now invite everyone to hold their coin in the palm of one hand. This penny is not very big. It won't buy very much. It sits here in your hand, and your hand is here in this church building. It's only a very little part of all the space in here. As you hold your penny, your hand is surrounded not just by the space of this building but by the whole universe. Now God is greater than the universe, because he is the One who thought and loved our universe into being.

There's a huge, huge difference between the kind of power and authority human leaders have, and the kind of power and authority God has. We are to give to God what is God's. What is God's? Is there anything God doesn't know? No. Is there anywhere God can't reach? No. Is there anything or anyone God doesn't care about? No. God is much greater and more wonderful than we can imagine, and he holds all creation in the palm of his hand, like you are holding the little penny in the palm of your hand.

No wonder we've all chosen to come and spend some time

praising him this morning! God is worth everything we can ever give him.

Of course, we are to respect our leaders, and keep the laws. We are to be good citizens, just as our Christian rule of love tells us. But we also need to remember who is ultimately in charge, and put God first. We need to be prepared to make a fuss if any laws are passed which are against God's law, and we need to do what we can to help our leaders uphold the authority of the God who made us all.

God's point of view

Ask for two volunteers. Stand one on a chair and have the other lie down on the floor. Talk with the volunteers about what they can see from their particular viewpoint. Although nothing else in the church has changed, the descriptions will be different because of where the volunteers are.

You could also suggest that everyone looks at something central, first through one eye and then the other. They can then all notice the change of view even when looking out from the same head!

We need to get into the habit of looking at everything from *God's* point of view. What we then see may sometimes come as a surprise to us, because we are so used to looking from our own point of view. Take Joseph, for instance (see Matthew 1:18-25). He was in for a surprise. He thought he had worked out the kindest way of dealing with the embarrassing problem of Mary expecting a baby before they were married. He had it all worked out. He'd divorce Mary without a big fuss, so that she needn't be noticed too much.

But through the dream God helped him look at things from another point of view. Joseph saw that Mary's baby was all part of God's plan, and, rather than divorcing her, he had an important job to do – to look after Mary and this very special baby. Joseph must have been a very brave man, as well as a good and kind one. He knew people would think he was stupid; perhaps they would stop being friends with him; his life would never be nice and straightforward again. But he did that brave, good thing because he had seen the situation from God's point of view and was happy to go along with that.

It was the same with Mary. If she had only seen the angel's message from her own point of view she might have refused to go along with God's plan, which was bound to turn her own hopes and dreams upside down. But she saw it from God's point of view – that the people of our earth needed a Saviour; God needed to be born as a human baby so he could rescue humans as an insider. And a baby needed a mum. So she agreed and that made Christmas possible.

God's warnings

Place around the church such warning signs as, 'Wet paint' on a chair, and 'Wet floor' next to a bucket and mop. Ask a couple of volunteers to go round the church to find the signs and bring them to you. Warnings are very useful! What would we do if we saw the 'Wet paint' sign? Avoid sitting on the chair. That's useful because it means our clothes don't get spoiled. What would we do if we saw the 'Wet floor' sign? We'd make a point of walking carefully, instead of running, so that we didn't slip on the wet floor and hurt ourselves.

It's quite normal for prophets to speak out God's warnings to his people, and Micah is no exception (see Micah 3:5-12). He doesn't mind that his message is going to be unpopular, any more than Jesus minds speaking out the truth. That's because he knows that warnings from God may help people sort out what is wrong in their life, say sorry to God for it, and ask his help to put things right as best they can. He tells his hearers the things they need to sort out and change. If they listen, and really start to repent, or turn their lives around, they will be able to work with God to put things right. Otherwise, they will end up with their holy city being destroyed.

Jesus warned his disciples that Jerusalem was going to be completely destroyed, even before some of them had died, because people had taken no notice of all the warnings they had been given (see Matthew 24:1-14). Jesus was talking in about AD 32, and over the next forty years all those earthquakes, wars and plagues happened in the area. In AD 70 the Romans stormed the city of Jerusalem and destroyed it completely, just as Jesus had foretold.

Warnings are useful, and we need to take notice of them. Some of us have been shown films to warn us about the dangers of smoking and drugs and AIDS, and we are warned each summer to protect our skin from sunburn. The captain on the *Titanic* was warned that too much speed could be dangerous. These warnings are there to help us, but we do need to listen to them and act on them if they are going to work.

It's just the same with our spiritual health and well-being. Show a torch and a ruler. God gives us his light to see by, and his truth to measure our lives by. If we become aware of God

warning us about our attitudes or behaviour or our relationships, we need to take it on board and do something about it
before it's too late.

God's practical help

Bring with you a small loaf of bread, a pillow, a calendar and a clock, writing paper and envelopes, and a briefcase. Place these prominently around the church.

Begin by reminding everyone of how our God hears us laughing and being happy, and is happy for us. He also hears us when we are crying and feeling sad, and his heart goes out to us, and he feels sad for us and quickly comes close to comfort us with his presence. Even if everyone else has let you down and rejected you, God never has and never will.

All of us will have some sad times in our lives, and today we are going to look at how God looks after his friends when they are going through a rough time. So even if you are in a really happy phase at the moment, it's a good idea to be prepared! And if today you are feeling a bit like Elijah (see 1 Kings 19:1-8), exhausted or chucked out, vulnerable and unable to see any hope, then God offers his help straight away.

Ask someone to go and find something to eat, and something to sleep on. As they go, explain how God is very practical, and starts by providing our practical needs – in this case, sleep and food. As the body of Christ, we church people can do that for one another.

Ask someone else to collect things to do with time. As they go, tell everyone that God gave Elijah time, and he didn't rush him. So we mustn't rush one another to get over a heartache either. People whose loved ones have died, or whose marriages are broken, for instance, need time, and we, in love, must give it to them, just as God does.

Ask someone to find some things for helping us keep in touch. While they are fetching them, talk about the way God was in contact with Elijah, and we are helped in our troubles if God's people make a point of keeping in contact through the dark days, and don't leave us feeling isolated. That's why sympathy and get-well cards, short visits and short phone calls can be so comforting. People need to know that we are all praying for them, too.

Ask someone to find something you might carry to work. As they collect it, talk about the way God knows when we are ready to move forward, and gives us a job to do. The job he gave the healed wild man in the Gospel today was to tell the people in the area about what God had done for him. Elijah was told to go back and continue his former work of being God's spokesman. The job God gives is one that only we can do, and it may well put to use the experiences we have suffered, so that they are turned into opportunities for good.

Leave all the objects out to remind people.

Listening to God

Begin by telling everyone you are going to drop a pin. Ask people to raise their hand if they hear it. (If the building is large, choose something slightly noisier to drop.) Point out how they all listened to be able to hear it. Today we are thinking about careful listening. Tell everyone you are going to drop the pin again, and this time ask them to notice what their bodies are doing to hear such a little sound. When you have dropped the pin, collect some of the things people have noticed. (These might include things like concentrating, waiting, being very still, cutting out our own noises, putting our best ear forward, turning our hearing aid up a bit.)

God is often revealed or shown to us through the scriptures – through the words in the Bible. (Hold a Bible and open it as you talk about it.) In Nehemiah 8:1-10 we hear how all the people gathered in the square in front of the temple and had God's law read out clearly to them so they could really understand it. And when they heard it like this, they couldn't wait to start living the way they knew God wanted them to live. The reason they heard God's voice that day was because they were really trying to listen, like us trying to hear the pin drop.

When Jesus went to preach at his local synagogue (see Luke 4:16-22) he taught the people that the prophecy from Isaiah was coming true that very day. The ones who were listening as carefully as you listened for the pin dropping would have been very excited. Jesus was giving them a very strong clue about who he really was. And it isn't every day you have the promised Messiah turning out to be someone you grew up with!

The trouble is that lots of them weren't listening at all. And in our lives we are often so busy and preoccupied with things that don't really matter that we make too much noise to hear the still, small voice of God telling us really important things about what is right and what is wrong, and how we can live good lives, full of honest, loving behaviour.

God will always whisper what is good and true and loving to help us. We won't hear an actual voice because God can speak straight into our hearts and minds, so we will just know, suddenly, that what we are doing is very good or very bad, very thoughtful or rather selfish and unkind. Once we know, we can stop the wrong behaviour and change it. But we do need to get used to listening so we can hear God clearly.

Peace with God

Ask everyone to place their hand flat on their tummy. This is often the place where we can tell if we are anxious or stressed, because it feels 'uptight'. When we are at peace, and not tensed-up, this place is where we feel calm and relaxed, and contented. (In fact, one way of calming yourself down is to do what you are doing now, and breathe slowly in and out a few times.)

Religion isn't telling God he is Lord of our life and then behaving as if he is not important. And it isn't going through the motions of worshipping him without showing his love and compassion to other people. It is all about being at peace with God. Ask for two people who are really good friends to come to the front, and talk to them about what it feels like to be with each other. How does being together make them feel? Do they feel worried about how the other friend will treat them? Would they trust their friend with a secret?

Best friends are good news. You are contented and happy to be with them, and are not worried all the time that you might say the wrong thing and offend them, or that they may start being nasty to you, so you need to be ready to hit them back if necessary. You know you can trust them with your secrets, and they won't laugh at you or think you are stupid. Even going through bad experiences isn't as bad if you are both in it together, because you know you will help one another along.

Well, that's what being at peace with God is like, and it has the spin-off effect of making us deeply happy and calm inside – a feeling that, whatever happens, all will be well. We heard today how Jesus wanted everyone to know this sense of calm assurance and peace and joy in their lives. He knew there were lots and lots of people going around worried and lost, with no peace inside them because they were not at peace with God. And he sent his disciples off to tell them that the kingdom of God was coming very soon, and soon they would be able to have that closeness with God which would give them peace.

Between the two 'best friends' put up a very large piece of cardboard with the word 'Sin' on it. Sin shuts us off from God and from one another. It makes us think of God as our enemy instead of our friend.

We know that Jesus went on to die for love of us all, which knocked that block of sin away between us and God. (Knock the cardboard away.) So now we can all know that lovely closeness to God which gives us real peace and hope, not just when everything is going well for us, but also through the times of suffering.

The unknown God

Start by displaying a fairly simple equation, such as $2x+3=x+10$, or $y(5+2)=21$, or $x+4=6$ (difficulty depends on your congregation), perhaps on a blackboard. Provide chalk, and ask someone mathematical to take us through the stages of solving the mystery of this unknown value of x or y.

When Paul was in Athens he saw an altar to 'the unknown god', and set about explaining to the people who this God was (see Acts 17:22-23). It was as if the people had been calling God 'x'. Now when we tried to solve our x mystery, we worked it out, step by step, gradually getting a clearer idea of what x meant, until, in the end, it was quite clear to us (or some of us!).

That's rather like the way we can look at the beauty and order of our world, and all the physics and chemistry of it, and all the variety and colour and shape in it, and begin to work our way towards discovering what God is like. We can work out that he must be clever and thoughtful, and imaginative and faithful, for instance.

But with Jesus coming, and showing us exactly what God is like, it's more like this.

Set up the same equation as before, using solid shapes, like building blocks. Each x is a bag, filled with the correct number of blocks. We could still work out what x is, but if the bag is opened, we can actually see what it is. (Do this.)

With Jesus' life there in front of us through reading the Gospels, and through living in his company every day, we can have a very clear idea of what God is like. We can see that he is forgiving and totally honest and good, that he is responsible and stands up for what is right, whatever happens to him and however much people sneer. We can see that he looks for the good in people and doesn't condemn them or give up on them. We can see that his love has been proved stronger than death.

If we put our faith in that God, whom Jesus has revealed to us in a new and clear way, and if we claim to love him, then we will have to start doing what he says. Who finds it easy to be obedient? Most of us find it very hard. We don't want to do what we are told; we want to do what we like!

Jesus says that the way you can tell if someone really does believe in him and love him, is by whether they are obedient to him, and obey what he says. That means listening to God and saying yes to him, whether it's what we want to do or not.

That is a *very hard* thing to learn, but it's worth learning, because being friends with Jesus is the best and happiest thing that could ever happen to us.

The stamp of God

Bring along a rubber stamp and ink pad, making sure it isn't permanent ink. Begin by putting the stamp on a number of volunteers. Talk about the way we sometimes get stamped at theme parks or discos to show that we have a right to be there because we have paid our entrance fee.

When we are baptised we have the sign of Jesus Christ marked on our foreheads. (What is that sign? It's the cross.) It's as if we've got God's stamp on us. (You could get everyone to trace a cross on their foreheads with their thumb to feel it freshly.) We are marked out as his children, whether we are one-day-old children, twenty-three-year-old children or ninety-seven-year-old children, and we have been freely given the right to belong in God's kingdom, which is a kingdom full of love and peace and joy, patience and kindness, goodness, gentleness and self-control.

As well as us belonging in God's kingdom, God's kingdom now belongs in us! As we've got God's stamp on us we will be wanting to behave like him, and he will help us to do that. Our behaviour will then be a visible sign to other people that we really do belong to God as his children. When they see us being honest and kind and patient and joyful, loving and working for peace and justice, they will be able to say, 'That must be a child of God – look how generous he is, even when he isn't going to gain anything by it!' And, 'That must be a child of God – look how loving she is with those difficult people!'

The whole point is this: we don't work to behave nicely so that God will love us. We don't need to do that, and we can't ever earn his love anyway. God simply loves us! He thinks we're really special, and he always wants the best for us.

When we love him back, and let him work in us, we will find we are beginning to behave more like our God. The closer we get to God, the more generous loving we will find ourselves doing. Instead of looking out for what we can get all the time, we'll find we're looking out eagerly for ways we can give instead! Instead of making sure we are doing whatever *we* want, we'll find we are looking to check if other people are OK. And that is actually a much happier and more fulfilling way to live.

God's harvest

Have ready a good supply of inflated balloons on strings. These will be needed later.

Bring out three sweets or apples and explain that three people are going to get them. Give them out completely randomly and then ask if that was fair. Agree with them that it wasn't fair, and often life seems unfair to us. (This is something that all ages know about.) Explain how our world is full of injustice and sometimes cruel and terrible things happen which don't make sense.

Now ask anyone who would like a balloon to raise a hand. Invite these people to come and collect a balloon and return to their seats. You will need them to gather with their balloons later on, when you beckon them.

As Christians we don't have to pretend the bad things aren't there, or try to work out easy answers that don't make sense. God knows there are sad and bad things happening in our world as well. They happened just the same when Jesus was walking around in Galilee. A tower fell on some people and killed them. The people asked Jesus to explain it, but he didn't. But he felt very, very sorry for anyone who was ill or whose child had died, and, instead of explaining why, he set about comforting them and doing everything he could to make things better. So that's what we need to do as well while we are alive.

But Jesus did tell us that life wouldn't always be unjust. One day, he said, everything as we know it will finish, and on that day everything you, and everyone else, have ever done which is good or kind, or helpful, friendly or honest will be gathered in, like harvest, and kept. (As you say this, gather all those with balloons together in the centre.) It will be an exciting and very beautiful harvest!

Let's make sure that we grow plenty of love and thoughtfulness and honesty and integrity in our lives, however old or young we are, so that whenever that last day comes, we'll be helping to make it a bumper harvest.

God's wonderful party

Bring with you a sealed envelope containing an invitation to a very special party or wedding. The date for the celebration needs to say 'to be arranged'.

Tell everyone how you have received this letter, and it looked so exciting that you thought you'd bring it to church and open it there. Invite someone to come and help you open the envelope, and someone a bit older to read it out. Show your excitement and start planning what to give as a present, and what to wear, getting suggestions from people and scribbling it all down on a list. Such a lot to think about!

Then stop as you ask to check the date of the celebration. Realise that it only says 'Date to be arranged'. *Date to be arranged!* That means you have no idea when to get ready. It might be ages to wait. It might be next week! Suppose it's next week!

Come to the conclusion that the only way you can be sure to be ready is to get ready straight away.

Put the invitation down and pick up a Bible. As you flick through the pages talk about how you are sure there is an invitation to a party somewhere in here as well. Find Isaiah 25:6-9 and read it out.

It's going to be quite a day, and we'll need to make sure we're ready for it. But what was the date again? Look and find it's another case of 'Date to be arranged'. Only God knows the actual date. That means it could be a long time ahead or it could be very close, so the best thing to do is to get ready straight away.

What kind of presents would be in order for this party?

Collect ideas like loving kindness, peacemaking, compassion, forgiveness, goodness and self-control. If we start now, we can grow those in our lives.

What kind of clothes would be suitable?

Clean clothes and good habits like honesty, faithfulness, humility, just or fair behaviour, and thoughtfulness. If we haven't got any yet, we can go to God's wardrobe and he'll make them to fit us perfectly. And if we have got them, but haven't worn them lately, now is the time to get them out and put them on again. These clothes get more and more beautiful as you wear them.

God's great day will be a wonderful celebration, and whether we are alive here or the other side of death, we will all be able to see it and take part.

JESUS OUR SAVIOUR

Jesus to the rescue

If you have a member of the congregation whose job involves rescue (for example in the fire, ambulance, lifeboat or mountain rescue services), ask if they would be willing to take part in a brief interview before the talk. Talk with them about the kind of dangers they themselves have to accept in order to rescue people, and the way they get alongside the people who need rescuing in order to help them. If you are not having a live interview, talk briefly about these rescuers.

Explain how Jesus is a rescuer, who comes in person to save us and help us. Stand someone on a paper island in the middle of a flood. God doesn't stand a long way off and shout to us. (Stand a long way off and shout to them to get into a boat and sail away.) That's no good, because the person feeling drowned by sadness or guilt or evil can't do what you are shouting even if they wanted to. We can't rescue ourselves; only God can set us free by accepting us, loving us and forgiving us. So instead of being a long way off and telling us what to do, God came in person to rescue us. (Pretend to row over to the person and then rescue them.) That's what happened at the first Christmas – God came to live among us in the person of Jesus, and he is still with us now. We are all his brothers and sisters.

Clothed in humanity

Beforehand cut out a simple white cloth tunic like this to fit a three- or four-year-old.

Invite a couple of toddlers and their parents to the front and interview them about the coats or jackets the children are wearing. Admire them and ask where they were bought, and what size was needed compared with their last coat.

Tell everyone how Samuel was brought to the temple when he was able to feed himself, and every year his mum brought him a new linen coat she had made. Every year he needed a slightly bigger one as he grew older. Produce your linen ephod lookalike and dress the toddler in it. As you do so, explain that it was worn as a sign of coming before God with a clean heart and mind. Priests all wore them, too.

When God came to earth as a baby, it was like him putting on the clothing of being human, and it was God's way of showing how much he loves us and is with us. It also helps us to see what God is like, because we cannot see God, but in Jesus we can see how God behaves. We can see that he enjoys people's company, wants to help them and shares their sadness and joy.

And Jesus didn't suddenly arrive on earth as a grown-up. He was born as a baby (draw attention to the size of someone very small in the congregation) and grew to be a toddler and a child (use other people of appropriate ages to demonstrate), so by the time he was a grown-up twelve-year-old he had experienced all the sort of human things that we experience.

Use the larger tunic with the word 'Humanity' written on it to clothe a twelve(ish)-year-old. All twelve-year-olds start asking questions about God and themselves, and so did Jesus. Part of wearing humanity meant that he developed as a human person and now he was grown-up he was fascinated to know who he was and why he was alive, just as we are. Those questions are important, and need to be asked. They are a sign of growing up. The answers for Jesus (and the answers for us) didn't come all at once. But his visit to the temple when he was twelve (see Luke 2:41-52) seems to have been a very important one for him. He began to understand that he was on earth to carry out God's purposes. That was why he was wearing the clothing of humanity. Perhaps for some of us, today is an important time for finding out God's purpose for us in our lives. We need to come into God's presence wearing the clothes of honesty and openness, and ask our questions.

Jesus is baptised

Ask various children if they know what job they would like to do when they grow up. Ask various adults what they wanted to be when they were children, and whether they did it or not. Ask some of the children if they have seen pictures of their mums and dads when they were babies and toddlers. Do they look anything like that now? Ask some of the mums and dads if they can imagine what their children will be like in twenty years' time.

Now let's look at Jesus (see Matthew 3:13-17). Here he is at about thirty years old. He's a carpenter, so he's probably quite strongly built. He's heard that his cousin, John (do they remember John?), is washing people in the River Jordan as a sign that God has forgiven their sins. We wash to get our bodies clean. John baptised people to show they were getting their souls clean. They were all getting ready for the Messiah, or Christ.

And now here comes Jesus, wading into the river, and wanting John to baptise him as well! (We know that Jesus is the Christ they were waiting for, but the people didn't know that yet.) John realises who Jesus is, and is shocked that he wants to be baptised. 'It ought to be the other way round!' says John. '*You* ought to be baptising *me*!'

Jesus insists. 'No, it's right for you to baptise me. God's work of putting things right all through the centuries is coming together now in this Baptism.' So John agrees to baptise Jesus. He pushes Jesus down under the water in the river, and when Jesus comes up out of the water, something amazing happens.

It's as if the heavens are opened up, and Jesus sees the Spirit of God coming to him and resting on him. Matthew tells us it looked something like a dove flying down to him. Jesus hears God his Father speaking to him deep into his being. God is saying that Jesus is indeed his well-loved Son, chosen and marked out for a special life that will save the world.

So that tiny baby, born in the stable, visited by shepherds and wise men, looked after by Joseph and Mary all through his childhood, is now at the start of his important work on earth. His job is to show the world God's love.

Resisting temptation

On matching sets of three graded sizes of card, from A5 to huge, write these two messages, with the print and thickness increasing with the card size.

I want it and I want it now.

Love God and love one another.

Begin by explaining that Jesus went into the desert after he had been baptised, and had a very hard time out there being tempted (see Luke 4:1-13). We all know what it feels like to be tempted. It's when we want something or want to do something which we know is wrong. (Show the middle-sized 'I want it and I want it now' card.) Ask someone to hold this card, but don't make them stand with their arms in the air for ages.

Jesus was being tempted to turn the stones into bread so he could eat them, but he knew that this would be using his power in a selfish way. He remembered that he loved God and he loved other people (display the largest 'Love God and love one another' sign). Ask someone else to hold this up.

As you can see, the love for God and other people stayed bigger than the temptation, and so Jesus was able to stand firm and not let the temptation get the better of him.

Whenever Jesus was tempted he always remembered that his love for God and other people was much stronger than the 'I want'. Put these signs down.

Now let's see what happens with us. First we get a little temptation inside us. (Give one helper the smallest 'I want' sign.) It isn't very big and we remember the right way to live (give the other helper the middle-sized 'Love God' sign) so we don't give way to the temptation.

But as we think about it more, this happens. (Exchange the small 'I want' for the middle-sized one.) And now there's a battle going on inside us, because the 'I want' is the same size as the 'Love God'. If we're not careful the 'I want' will get even bigger! (Swap it for the largest 'I want' sign.) And when we let the 'I want' get bigger than the 'Love God', even for a minute, we're in danger of falling into temptation, and doing or saying what we really know is wrong.

Jesus shows us how to do this. As soon as you feel a little

'I want' coming on (show it), remember that you love God and you love other people more than you want what is wrong. (Display the middle-sized 'Love God' sign.) And if the 'I want' gets bigger in you (show the middle-sized 'I want') think hard about how you and God love each other (show the largest 'Love God' sign) so that the 'I want' is less strong and you can fight it; and instead of giving in and doing or saying what you know is wrong, God will be helping you to stand up to temptation and win.

Who is Jesus?

Beforehand, ask a few people of different ages to provide you with a photograph of them when they were very young, and have these pictures duplicated, or shown on an OHP. Don't identify them, but say they are all members of the church community. When people have had a go at guessing the identities, ask the people to come to the front. This narrows the choice, and makes it easier to see who's who. We might have a hunch about someone, and can ask them directly. They will tell us whether or not we are right, and then we'll know for certain. (Invite people to do this.) Once we know the true identity, it's often easier to see the likeness!

Jesus knew that people had all sorts of ideas about who he was (see Matthew 16:13-17). Some ideas were close to the truth, some were wide of the mark, and Jesus always wanted his followers to make the discovery for themselves. Discovering something for ourselves means that we always remember it far better than when we have simply been told things. (People may remember discovering for themselves that fire burns, for instance, that cement hardens into a solid lump, or that overloading a computer can cause it to crash.)

No doubt Jesus sensed that the disciples had almost got to the point of discovering that he was not just their friend and teacher, but also the promised Messiah, the Son of God. This conversation, starting with what other people think, will help them tip over into that 'Aha!' of learning, that point when you suddenly know something and everything falls clearly into place.

It is Simon, the fisherman, who comes out with it for the first time. 'You are the Christ,' he says, 'the Son of the living God.' It must have been a bit like when you first say the words 'I love you' or 'I'm three'. It's the first time you have ever said it and as you say it, you know it is really true, and your life will never be quite the same again.

The water of life

You will need some paper cups, one with holes poked in it, a washing-up bowl or bucket and a jug of water.

Remind everyone of the way the people in the desert were very thirsty, and Moses asked God how their thirst could be quenched (see Exodus 17:1-7). He also told God how grumpy everyone was getting – they were so grumpy that Moses began to think they might take their anger out on him physically! God answered by providing water tumbling out of a rock, fresh and pure and delicious. There's nothing more wonderful when you're thirsty than the refreshing sound and taste of water. Now pour some water out and enjoy the sound of it. Invite some thirsty person to drink some from the proper cup. The people wanted to be back in the past, but God wanted to lead them on into the future.

John 4:5-15 tells us about two more water supplies. One was a well, where a woman had come to collect water, and where Jesus was sitting, feeling thirsty. Perhaps his own thirst reminded him of the people getting grumpy with Moses in the desert, and the way God had given them the flowing, living water they needed.

The other water supply is a bit unusual. Jesus told the woman about some water which would quench her thirst completely, and become a spring of water inside her welling up to give her life that lasts for ever. At first the woman thought this sounded too good to be true! What Jesus was doing was explaining the way God fills our lives, and leads us into the future, satisfying us all the way along, and refreshing us when we are sad and longing for good and right and fair and helpful things to happen in our world. The more we go to God to be filled with his living water of life and love, the more we shall find that we too are becoming sources of love and comfort and fairness and truthfulness for other people.

Let's see what happens when we pour some water into this cup with holes in it. (Station some people around with proper cups.) Pretend this hol(e)y cup is a Christian drinking the living water of life and love from the living, loving God. Can you see how the Christian then pours out that love to other people he or she meets? There's no problem that God will suddenly dry up, because God is living, flowing, for ever. And the other people may well want to become hol(e)y themselves, drinking that eternal supply which they can see is changing us for the better.

So if your life feels rather dry or thirsty or stuck in the past, go to Jesus; keep going to Jesus; and let him fill you up with the living spiritual water that really satisfies. And don't keep it all to yourself – pass it on!

The Good Shepherd

Using chairs, build a circular sheepfold, with a gap for the entrance. Ask for some volunteer sheep to go inside. Explain that this is what a sheepfold was like in Jesus' day, except that it was made of stones, not chairs. Is there a door? No, there isn't. That's because the shepherd himself was the door. Ask a volunteer shepherd to come and be the door of the sheepfold. (You could even give the shepherd a stick or crook from the Nativity costumes, and a shepherd's sling.) Why is this living door likely to be a good safe one for the sheep? Because the shepherd would hear any dangers, such as wolves, or bears, or sheep stealers, and take action to protect the sheep, using his staff or sling. (The shepherd can pretend to frighten off a dangerous wolf.)

Another thing about sheep is that they get very frightened by lots of things, but when they hear the voice of the shepherd at the door they know they can trust him, and they feel safe. They will even follow him when he calls them and leads them off to some good juicy grass. (The sheep can try this.) And then they will follow the shepherd back home at the end of the day. (They do this.)

Now why are we getting a lesson in sheep farming this morning? What has all this got to do with Jesus? Or us?

In John 10:7-15 we hear Jesus telling the people that he is the sheep-door. (And you know what that means, now.) He told them all about the sheep being safe when the shepherd is the door, and the sheep knowing the shepherd's voice and following him. (You know about that too.) But the people didn't have a clue why Jesus was talking to them about sheep and shepherds. So they asked him to explain.

Jesus said he was trying to tell them something important about God. (Can anyone think what it was?) He was telling the people that they were a bit like sheep and Jesus was like the good shepherd who lies down in the doorway to keep the sheep safe. He was saying that God looks after us and defends us with his life because he loves us so much. He hates the thought of us coming to harm, and fights off evil. We can trust God's voice when he calls us, and follow him without any fear because we know God is always faithful and good and loving.

So whenever you are scared to face a bad problem, or bad ideas and temptations keep coming at you, stand there in the sheepfold behind Jesus, the sheep-door, and you will be safe. And whenever you are muddled about whether to do something or not, or whether to be selfish or not, listen out for the quiet calling of the Good Shepherd (you won't hear it with your ears, but you will know it in yourself) and follow him into the way that is right and good and kind and loving.

The Way, the Truth and the Life

Ask two or three experts to come and explain the way they do whatever it is they are good at. (The actual areas of expertise depend on the interests of your congregation, but try and choose people from representative age and interest groups. The skill should be capable of being demonstrated in front of everyone, so it could be ironing, juggling, dribbling a football, doing a cartwheel or skipping, for example.)

First ask each one to explain it to you, placing them out of sight of everyone as they do so. Share with the congregation how it all sounds incredibly complicated, and difficult to follow, even though it is obviously expert advice. That's rather how it is with the Old Testament Law – everyone respects it highly and it's very good advice for living, but somehow we never seem to manage to follow the instructions or get the hang of them. They help us to know how to live a good life, but they don't change us so that we are able to do it. Some of the prophets had told everyone that one day it would be different. People wouldn't need those instructions any more, because they would already know, in their hearts, how to behave properly.

Let's find out if we can understand our experts any better if we can actually see them doing these clever things. (Invite them to demonstrate, one by one.) Ah, that's much clearer! We may not be able to do it ourselves, yet, but at least we have their example in front of us, to learn from and copy. (Someone might like to try copying one of the skills.)

When Jesus came, it was like being able to see God's way of living – in person. 'So that's what it means to love God and love one another!' people thought. 'So that's what God's love for us is like!' And even though we may not yet be able to do it very well, at least we have a wonderful example to learn from and copy.

If we're still full of bitterness about something that happened to us long ago, we can look at Jesus and copy his forgiving. If we're looking down on someone because they aren't as clever or rich as us, we can look at Jesus and copy his way of enjoying people and accepting them for what they are. If we are always worrying about clothes and possessions, we can look at Jesus and copy his simple way of living, and spend our energy cultivating the treasures that we can take with us to heaven. So Jesus is like a living 'Way' – he's a walking, talking Way to live.

In fact that's what Jesus called himself in John 14:6; he said, 'I am the Way, the Truth and the Life'. With Jesus we go one better than having his example to copy – since the Resurrection we can have his life living in us! That would be rather like our experts being able to fill us with all that makes them able to do those clever things. Imagine what a skilled church we would be if that were possible! We'd all be expert ironers, football dribblers, jugglers and cartwheelers! Well, I have to tell you that we can't do that. As humans we have to pass on our skills the hard way, by teaching and learning. But with Jesus it's different. He really can live in our lives, enabling us to love God and one another. All we need to do is invite him into our personal lives and our church, and be prepared to be gradually transformed.

The Servant King

Bring along a crown and robe, some pretend bags of money, a dish of fruit and two fans on sticks as shown below. Drape some cloth over a chair.

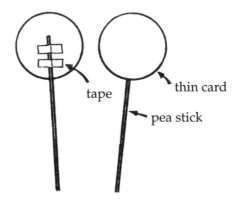

Tell everyone that today we are celebrating that Jesus Christ is King for ever. Ask a volunteer to come out and dress them up in the grand robe of very costly material, hand-embroidered by expert craftsmen, and the solid gold crown, studded with real diamonds and rubies. Sit the king on a grand throne covered in pure silk and made from finest marble, and provide him with some servants to stand around and wave him with fans, bowing before him. Give him bags of money on a table nearby, and provide a dish of fresh fruits for him to snack on between banquets.

Is this right? Is this what King Jesus is really like? No, it's all wrong! Although Jesus has been given all power and majesty and honour, and is King of all time and space, he is a very different sort of king. He lays aside his majesty (help the king up from his throne), lays aside his robe and his crown (take them from him), lays aside all wealth and comfort (the servants move the table), so that he can be one with us (he shakes hands with the servants) and live among us, caring for us, searching for the lost, and binding up the injured. (Thank the servant and the king for their help.)

Now if that's how our king behaves, then that's how we are to behave as well. If we worship and honour a Servant King, who doesn't greedily look after his own needs all the time but makes a point of looking after other people's needs, then that's what we have to do! Our wealth and treasure will be in loving service, wherever we're needed. That's how Jesus will recognise us as his people, when we get to the gate of heaven.

Transfiguration

Bring along a family photograph album with snaps of holidays or celebrations in it, and if possible a camera which takes instant pictures. Also have two cards to hold up, one with a large plus sign on and the other a large minus sign.

If you have an instant camera, begin by taking a picture of some people or the day's flower arrangement. Show the album and talk about the way we all like to snap away to capture the moments when we are on holiday or at a special celebration, or when our children and grandchildren are growing up. We want to hang on to the moment and cherish it for years to come, because we know the moment itself won't last. The children will soon grow up, and we may never have the chance to visit the Eiffel Tower or Southend illuminations ever again!

The 'plus' side of taking pictures like this (encourage everyone's suggestions) may be that we will remember better if we look back at the picture – it may help us see the importance of the occasion, it helps us pass on the family tradition to the next generation, and it lets us enjoy more at our leisure later than we were able to take in at the time.

The 'minus' side may be that we're so busy taking pictures at the time that we aren't able to concentrate properly on the actual moment.

In Matthew 17:1-9 we hear about something amazing which happened on a mountain in Galilee. Three of Jesus' friends – Peter, James and John – saw Jesus shining with God's glory as he prayed. It was one of those times when Peter wanted to reach for the camera (except that cameras hadn't been invented then) so they could hold on to the wonderful moment for ever. Perhaps they had never before felt God quite so close to them! They even heard God's voice. He wasn't saying, 'I hope you're watching carefully and I'm sorry cameras haven't been invented yet or you could have got a pretty dramatic picture here today!' He was helping them understand the real, actual experience they were in, assuring them that Jesus really was God's Son, and wanting them to listen to Jesus in a way they had never listened before.

God doesn't just want Peter, James and John to know – he

wants St Peter's church and St James's and St John's and all the other churches to know. He wants all the people in all the world to know who Jesus is, and he wants us all to pay attention to what Jesus says, and really listen to him with our hearts and minds as well as our ears.

Jesus shows us God

Ask a volunteer to stand at the front, holding a large piece of card in front of them so that no one can see their face. Point out that we can't be certain whether the person is looking happy, sad or angry, because we can't see for ourselves. Ask the volunteer to make one of those expressions behind the card. We can talk to them and listen to them, but we can't see them. It was a little like that for the people of Israel. Sometimes the prophets would speak out God's word to them, and they prayed to God, but it wasn't until Jesus came that people could see what God was like.

(Take the card from the volunteer's face.) We can now see clearly whether the person is happy, sad or angry, and we can see how s/he behaves, and what s/he thinks is important. When Jesus came to live as a human being on our earth, walking about in the actual place of Galilee and in the actual time of Roman-occupied Palestine, people could see exactly what God thought was important, and how much he loved them.

They saw that God really is interested in our everyday worries such as having enough food, or enough time or energy to get our work done.

They saw that God goes on loving us right to the very limit and still carries on loving! (Jesus went on loving and forgiving right through being put to death on a cross.)

They saw that God likes to work with us in solving some of our problems, and, if we are happy to work with him, amazing things can happen.

There will be lots of times this week when we can choose to do 'exactly what Jesus tells us' and, if we agree, God will be able to use us in providing lovingly for someone's needs. Perhaps we will be giving our complete attention to someone when they talk to us, or providing financial help or emotional support. Perhaps our smile will cheer someone up, or our help will give someone a well-needed rest. Perhaps by letting someone play we will be making them feel less lonely and happier. Perhaps the spare curtains we remember to take into the charity shop will be exactly what someone is hoping to find as they struggle to furnish a home with very little money.

Let's make sure that this week we listen out for the ways

God asks for our help, and then do what he whispers in our hearts, so that the people in this town can actually see God's love in action.

Putting things together

Bring in some kind of game or piece of equipment which needs putting together and setting up properly before it can be used. This could be anything from a computer to a folding bed – it all depends on what is available and the interest area of the congregation. It needs to have a set of instructions to go with it.

Begin by introducing your item of equipment. Pretend that you are having a real problem with this thing because you don't understand it at all. You don't understand how to get it to work.

Have a primed helper who comes up at this stage and shows you the instruction leaflet. They tell you that if you read that it will tell you how the thing works and how to use it. Be surprised, but set to reading some of the instructions, without relating them to the equipment. They don't make much sense to you, and you get fed up. It's no good – you don't understand and it doesn't make sense.

Explain that this is rather like the way the two disciples felt as they walked sadly back home on the very first Easter Day (see Luke 24:13-35). They didn't understand anything any more. They had great hopes about Jesus, but now he was dead, so their hopes were dead as well. They had heard about the women saying they had seen Jesus alive early that morning, but that didn't make any sense to them either. How on earth could someone be dead as dead and now be alive? It couldn't possibly be true!

Just then someone joined them and asked what they were so sad about. And when they told him, he started to show them how it actually did make a lot of sense. (Break off as the helper comes and offers to take you through the instructions and sort the equipment out. Accept their help and marvel as gradually, step by step, it starts to come together, and eventually works. Be excited about this and thank the helper. Then come back to the Emmaus story.)

Well, it certainly helps to have someone who really understands to help you when you are in a muddle! That's how those disciples felt when the stranger explained that it was all there in the scriptures (pick up a Bible) about the promised Messiah having to suffer and die before there could be new life. When they reached their home they invited the helpful stranger in to stay with them, and when their guest took the bread and blessed and broke it (mime this) . . . what do you think they suddenly realised?

It was Jesus!

And that is still what Jesus does. He walks along with us where we are walking. He helps us understand about God through the words of scripture (pick up the Bible again), he helps us make sense of life and its problems (stand beside the working piece of equipment), and he makes himself known to us in the breaking of bread.

Goodbye?

Begin by talking about saying goodbye. The kind of goodbye it is depends on how well we know each other, whether we love or hate each other, and whether we are saying goodbye for a short time, a long time or for ever. In Acts 1:6-11 we see the disciples as Jesus says goodbye to them. Since Easter he had been meeting up with them after the Resurrection. Sometimes he had met them when they were all together, sometimes on their own. They would suddenly recognise him, or he would suddenly be there among them, and the disciples had begun to get used to Jesus being with them even when they couldn't see him with their eyes.

Now, here they are, all together with Jesus, and this is going to be their last goodbye to him as a person whom they see with their eyes, because he is going back to heaven. He tells them two things: (show a picture of rushing wind and flames) that they are going to be given power when the Holy Spirit comes upon them, and (show a picture of an empty speech bubble) that they are going to tell lots of people all over the world about the Jesus they know and love so well.

Then we are told that he was lifted up, while they watched, and a cloud took him from their sight so that they couldn't see him any more. So they stood there, peering up into the sky, rather like you do when you've just let a balloon go, and you watch and watch until you can't see it any more. What happened next?

They realised that two people, dressed in white, were standing next to them. 'Why are you standing here looking up into the sky?' they asked. They told the disciples that one day Jesus would come in the same way they had seen him go. But what they wanted them to know was that there wasn't any point in hanging around in that one place for a glimpse of Jesus, because he had gone on to the next phase, where he would be with all his friends, including us, all the time, not in a way that we can see, but in new ways. Just as real, just as much alive, but in a form which makes him free to be in all kinds of different countries and places and dates and times all at once!

What he said to the disciples that day, he says to us as well: we will be given power when the Holy Spirit comes upon us (show the first picture again) and we are going to tell lots of people about the Jesus we know and love (show the second picture).

A hero's welcome

Beforehand ask a few people to bring awards they have been given. These should include things that probably lots of others have as well, such as a five-metre swimming badge and a driving licence. There may also be a darts cup or a music certificate.

Begin by showing the awards and talking briefly to the award-holders about how these have been well earned, and give us an idea of the standard that has been achieved, so they are something to celebrate. Probably lots of us have similar awards that we have been honoured with, which is well worth celebrating. (A round of applause may be in order.)

When Jesus entered heaven, about forty days after he had come back to life on the first Easter Day, the whole of heaven gave him a hero's welcome. They said he was worthy to receive power and wealth and wisdom and strength, honour and glory and praise – everything good they could think of.

They wanted to honour him like this because Jesus had managed to do such an incredible thing. He had lived a human life and gone on loving all the way through it without once giving in to temptation, turning against God's will or putting his own wants first. Through loving people enough to die for them, he had been able to break the hold death has over all of us, so we can live freely and happily in God's company. (Another huge round of applause for Jesus.)

Now go back to the swimming badge. This badge proves that Susie is able to swim. What God is saying to us today is that Jesus has won the victory for us, so we are all able to live this incredible new, free and happy life in his company.

It is as if there's a wonderful pool just waiting for us to enjoy, but perhaps we're only holding our badges at the edge of the pool, instead of getting into the water and using them. Let's plunge into the life Jesus has won for us and enjoy it to the full!

THE HOLY SPIRIT

The fire of the Spirit

Beforehand make five red, yellow and orange flame shapes (about 30 centimetres high) and hide them around the church.

Begin by asking for examples of flames, such as on a gas hob, bonfire, forest fire, log fire, candle, acetylene torch, fire-eater, house on fire, match, oil lamp, steel works, steam engine, lighter, Bunsen burner. Draw people's attention to the tremendous power of some of these and the quiet, gentle nature and soft light of others. Fire is something we all have to respect, as it can burn and destroy as well as giving us light and heat.

Send the children off to search for the five flames that are hidden in the church, and tell the adults about our need to seek out the Spirit expecting to find, just as the children are doing now. They trust that what they have been told to search for will be there, and it will. We need to believe that if we seek God we will find him – and we will.

When the children return with the five flames, you can remind everyone of the way the Holy Spirit is described as being like tongues of fire, with the sound of a rushing wind. (You can get everyone to make this sound as the flame-carriers run round the church.)

Like fire, the Spirit can be strong and powerful in our lives. (The first flame is held up.) Sometimes the Spirit is gentle and quiet, whispering deep into our needs and telling us what is right. (The second flame is held up.) Like fire, the Spirit is warming, spreading love and a real desire to put things right, and stand up for goodness and truth. (The third flame is held up.) Like fire the Spirit is purifying, burning away all that is evil and selfish in us, so that we can become like pure refined gold, glowing with the light of God's love. (The fourth flame is held up.) And, like fire, the Spirit is enlightening, shedding light for us on the Bible, our conversations and relationships and the events of our lives, so that we can see God more clearly through them. (The fifth flame is held up.)

The wind of the Spirit

You will need a hand-held hairdryer (and possibly an extension lead).

Begin by talking about the wind, and how we can tell it is windy, even though the wind itself is invisible. Collect examples of the signs from the congregation. Draw together the signs with the principle that wind makes things move.

Now ask some volunteers to scatter some cut-out paper people on the ground, fixing some firmly to the ground with blutack or paperweights. In John 3:1-8 we overhear a conversation between Jesus and a man called Nicodemus. We know Nicodemus was a Pharisee, and knew lots of clever things. But Jesus puzzled him. He could see that the miracles Jesus was doing made it look as if Jesus really was God's promised Messiah who they were all waiting for. The problem was, Jesus didn't seem to be sticking rigidly to the rules Nicodemus and the other Pharisees felt he ought to be. He seemed far too broad-minded. He was spending time with sinners.

The good thing about Nicodemus was that he didn't keep his worries to himself, or pretend they weren't there, or reject Jesus because he was making him think about things in a new way. He went to find Jesus one night and talked to him about it all. And that's what we need to do with all our doubts and puzzles and questions.

Jesus gave him some funny answers, and one of the answers was about the wind. He said that living in the Spirit is rather like being blown by the wind. God wants to move us along and he can do that so long as we don't fix ourselves down. Watch how the wind from the hairdryer can move these people. (Switch on the hairdryer and blow the people along.)

Look at these people who were stuck down to the floor. The wind blew but they haven't moved anywhere. And sometimes we are like that. We might sing on Sundays about wanting to live in God's Spirit, but when that means being ready to move or change in our life or our attitudes or ideas, we start fixing ourselves to the floor where we feel safer, and can enjoy moving a little to the breath of God, but not enough to be actually moved along.

So let's work at being brave enough to come to Jesus with

the deep worries and puzzles of life, knowing that God is quite able to cope with them and won't suddenly disappear or be offended. And let's work at being brave enough to stand out in the wind of God's Spirit, without fixing ourselves to the spot, but willing for him to move us as a church and as individuals wherever he wants to move us.

Filled with the Holy Spirit

Bring with you something to inflate, such as a beach ball, or a travel neck-cushion, or a balloon.

Begin by playing a snippet of *When the saints go marching in*, reminding everyone of all the saints who have gone marching into heaven, and we also want to be among that number one day.

But what is a saint? You may have some windows with particular saints on. If so, you can briefly draw people's attention to these, and any saintly connections your church or town has. Emphasise that although these may be importantly fixed in stained glass now, in their lives they were ordinary people. We may well have lots of saints sitting here now, because we are *all* called to be saints, or God's holy people.

How can you spot a holy person when you meet one? The way they think and talk and behave makes you realise that they are full of God's loving Spirit. Show your inflatable. It was designed to be full of air, so at the moment, without air in it, it isn't really able to be properly itself. Ask someone to breathe into it to inflate it. Can we see the air that has been breathed in? No. Can we see the difference it makes? Yes! It has turned this ball/cushion/balloon into what it was designed to be, so now it is really itself, and also very useful.

We can't see the loving Spirit of God either. But whenever people are filled with it, they are able to be more fully their true selves, and it shows in their love for God and their love for others. Lots of inflatables have a valve which stops the air coming in until it is deliberately opened. With us, too, there has to be a definite decision to open up to God's in-breathing of his Spirit. What the saints have done and are doing is keeping that valve open, so that they can be filled with the Spirit, and topped up whenever they get a bit deflated.

One saint – Paul – wrote about the whole church being filled with the Holy Spirit of God. The Church isn't supposed to have loads of deflated Christians and one or two saints here and there who are full of God's loving Spirit. The idea of the church is that *everyone* in it is full of the breath of God!

Let God fill you up with his life, and make you into the person he knows you can be. We'll all look different shapes, and we'll all be useful to the world in different ways, just as a beachball is useful for throwing around but not so good as a pillow or a camping mattress. But as God breathes his loving Spirit into us more and more, we will become more and more our true selves – holy people the world needs, marching into God's kingdom with all the other saints.

Guided by the Spirit

First fill the space of the centre aisle with chairs and obstacles. If yours is a fixed pews building, have people to sit down as obstacles in the aisle. Remind everyone of how Jesus was talking to his friends at the last supper they had together before he was crucified. Jesus knew his friends were dreading the future without him being there with them. Perhaps they thought it would be a bit like this.

Ask for a volunteer and blindfold them, twizzle them round and send them off down the aisle. As they walk hesitantly, bumping into the obstacles, you talk about Jesus' friends thinking that living without Jesus around would be like trying to get round the difficulties of life blindfolded, and with no one to help or guide them.

Rescue the volunteer and remove their blindfold. As this person knows, you don't feel very safe all on your own and unable to see where the obstacles are. It is frightening and could be dangerous. Sometimes our life can feel like that, and it isn't a comfortable place to be.

What Jesus wants his friends to know is that God doesn't have that in mind for them at all. Although Jesus knew he wouldn't be there physically with his friends for ever, he promised them that they (and we) would have a personal guide right there with us. Let's see how that changes things for us.

Blindfold the volunteer again, but this time appoint a sensible, caring guide who steers them round the obstacles, talking to them and helping them along. (You may want to have primed this person beforehand.)

Watch them together, and then talk alongside the rest of their journey about God's Holy Spirit being with us to teach and explain things to us, to guide us and help us through the dangerous parts of life, so that we are not left alone, but working in partnership with our loving God.

Following Jesus

Total commitment Olga Korbut.

You will need someone who can do gymnastics or dance. Ask them to prepare a sequence of moves which need total commitment in order to work, such as somersaults and cartwheels, pirouettes and arabesques.

Begin by asking the gymnasts or dancers to perform their demonstration. Briefly interview them, thanking them and asking whether they could do these things first time, or whether they had to practise. Draw attention to the commitment that has to be given to anything you want to do really well. You can't 'half do' some of those moves, or you'd probably fall flat on your face.

As Christians we are called to that same kind of commitment. We can't 'half do' it. When we commit ourselves to following Christ, it's going to affect the way we talk, the way we behave with our friends and our enemies, the way we spend our time and our money. It's going to affect all our thinking and the choices we make. So it's a bit like deciding to do a double somersault, or a triple pirouette – it takes a lot of dedication and courage to launch off.

Imagine if you were just launching yourself into a triple somersault and all your strength suddenly wasn't there. You'd certainly notice it was missing! In fact, you wouldn't be able to do any of those clever moves without strength.

In our Christian life, God's Holy Spirit is the strength. He enables us to do those triple somersaults of caring love for those we don't much like, and the double pirouettes of co-operating when all we want is our own way. Real loving is very hard work, and it takes lots of dedication. With God's strength we can do it, and then we will be moving freely and beautifully through life, in the way God called us to, and knows will make us, and others, truly happy.

Baptism

Using a flipchart, OHP or large sheet of paper and thick pens, collect everyone's suggestions about what water can do. Some of the suggestions can be drawn rather than written, so that the non-readers can also join in.

Read through all the suggestions to celebrate them, and talk about how Baptism picks up on these qualities of water and uses them to teach us spiritual things. When we are baptised we are 'drowned' to the old ways, given new life, washed clean, and refreshed. If it is practical, have water in the font and pour it as you explain each quality and its spiritual meaning.

Remind everyone about Jesus being baptised, and how, as he was praying, the Holy Spirit came upon him, looking rather like a dove flying down to rest on him. And God told Jesus that he was God's Son, and God was well pleased with him.

Point out any dove symbols there are in the church – in carvings, pictures or windows – and have a cut-out dove shape (you can use the picture below) to show everyone. The dove has become a sign or symbol for the Holy Spirit because of what happened at the Baptism of Jesus.

When we are baptised God calls us actually by name to follow him, and sets us apart to love and serve him through the whole of our life. We can only do that with the gift of the Holy Spirit, so that is what we are given. The more we use it, the more it will grow. The sign of the dove will remind us. Whenever we see a dove or a pigeon, or a wild goose, it will remind us that we belong to God, and have chosen to follow him.

Seeing ourselves

You will need a mirror. First do a spot of face-painting on a volunteer, writing their own name in mirror-writing across their face. Then show them their face in the mirror. They will be surprised at what they look like because it isn't their familiar face looking back at them. Yet it is their own named self they are looking at.

Whenever Jesus met up with people he seems to have been able to show them who they were; what they were really like. By the things he said, the stories he told, and by the signs and miracles he did, people were able to look at him and suddenly see something about themselves they hadn't realised before. Some suddenly realised that they were lovable and important, when they had always thought they were rubbish. Others suddenly saw that they were living very mean, selfish lives, and knew they wanted to change.

In the story told in Luke 5:1-11, Simon Peter has been fishing all night long without any success at all. It's possible that Jesus had watched them, and noticed how they carried on even when they were tired and disappointed. Perhaps Jesus brought that into his teaching, and the fishermen would have sat up on the beach and thought, 'This man really knows what it's like to be a fisherman like me, working all night with nothing to show for it!' So when Jesus suggested they try again, Simon was doubtful, but willing to give it a go. The huge catch of fish, coming suddenly after all that time they had worked in vain, must have given Simon a shock. It was a bit like looking in a mirror and seeing who he really was for the first time.

He saw that this man Jesus, who had been sitting in Simon's own fishing boat talking to the crowds, was different from anyone he had ever met before. His goodness, his wise teaching and his knowledge of where the fish were, all made Simon suddenly ashamed. We don't know what it was in Simon's life that went through his mind. It might have been some particular sin he still felt guilty about, or it might have been remembering all the general meanness and selfishness, or the bad temper he knew he had.

The important thing for us to look at is how Jesus helped him see himself, and then said, 'Don't be afraid, follow me.'

That is what Jesus does with us today as well. So be ready for it. If something makes you suddenly see yourself and you don't like everything you see, Jesus will not be standing at your elbow, saying, 'There's no hope for you, then, is there? You might as well give up.' He will be there, speaking into your heart words of love and comfort and hope: 'Don't be afraid of what you really are. Come and follow me.'

Ready for the race?

Beforehand prepare a number of heavy carrier bags and a rucksack, and have a sack or strong dustbin bag. Label the bags 'I want my own way', 'It isn't fair', 'So what?', 'I'll never forgive them' and 'No one will notice'. Also bring the local school's PE kit.

Begin by showing everyone the PE kit and draw from them what it is, who wears it, and why we do PE dressed like this instead of in our best clothes, or in bridesmaids' dresses, or Mickey Mouse suits. Establish that it's more practical and comfortable to wear light clothes like this which don't get in the way of our running and jumping.

Refer to the letter to the Hebrew Christians (see Hebrews 12:1-2) in which following Jesus through our lives is said to be a bit like running a race: we need to look where we're going. That means keeping our eyes on Jesus and his way of living. This will keep us on the right track in our own lives, reminding us to be honest instead of telling lies, thinking of other people's needs instead of just wanting our own way, and sharing our ideas and fears with God instead of ignoring him most of the time.

But often we run our Christian life in very unsuitable clothes. At this point ask for a volunteer, and load them up with all the bags, explaining what each represents, and how we weigh ourselves down with all this luggage. As you hand over the sack for them to stand in, point out how difficult we make it for ourselves by hanging on to all these attitudes which make Christian living extra hard. The volunteer can try running to prove the point.

Today we are being given a useful tip for Christian living: get rid of all these unhelpful habits (name them as you take them from the volunteer), so that we are free to run God's race-track uncluttered and 'light'. Then we can concentrate on Jesus, and learn to live his way – the way of love.

Spreading the good news

Bring with you a newspaper, a TV remote control, a mobile phone, an airmail letter and, if possible, a trumpeter (failing a real one, a recorded version will do nicely).

Begin by picking up the newspaper and reading out a few headlines. Talk about this being one of the ways we use to get other people to hear our news. People used to use a town crier. (You could ask a loud-voiced volunteer to demonstrate. The news they bellow is written on a piece of paper: 'There is only one real God. He made us and he loves us!') Pick up the remote control and explain that now we don't have to shout so loud because we invite the town criers into our homes and sit them in the corner to tell us the latest news. We can even switch them off!

Another thing people used was a trumpeter. (Have this demonstrated briefly.) That got people's attention so they would listen to what you were saying. Now we have this to get people's attention, and get them listening to us. (Demonstrate the mobile phone.) People used to send their news by pigeons, and now we send it on a metal bird. (Show the airmail letter.)

What has stayed the same all through the years is that people always want to pass on their news. And in Romans 10:9-15 we are told that the news the town crier shouted to us (they can do it again) is such good news, not just for us but for everyone, that we need to make sure we pass it on. Like honey or peanut butter, we are not to keep the good news to ourselves, but spread it!

We can tell people about God's love by behaving in a kind and loving way, by being generous with our time and money, by praying for our friends and for difficult situations, by living by God's rules, and by bringing our faith into the conversation instead of only mentioning it among our church friends. And who knows, God may also call some of you to tell the good news as newspaper reporters, in government, on television or as a famous sports star. However you do it, do it!

Prayer and Bible study

Bring along (or ask someone else in the congregation to bring) something which you have made or are making, which requires lots of persistence and perseverance (such as a garment or model, diary or recipe). Talk about the struggle you have had keeping going with it. Use parts of the church building, particularly if it is an ancient one, and draw everyone's attention to some piece of stained glass or carving, and all the persistence and hard work that went into making it. Emphasise the value of doing these things, even though they are difficult.

Jesus tells us to keep going with our prayer, and never give up. Suggest a pattern of praying when you wake up, before you eat a meal, and before you go to sleep at night, showing large posters of logos for these (as below). Or they can be shown on an OHP. If we get into a prayer habit like this, we will be deepening our friendship with God, and getting to know him better.

There is another good habit we need to have as well as praying, and that is reading the Bible every day. There are lots of books and schemes to help us, and we can choose one which suits our age, interests and experience. If we don't know much about the Bible there are people in the church to talk it over with.

However we read it, it's important to pray and read God's word in Scripture so that we really can have God's law of love remembered in our minds and written on our hearts. That way we will be ready for any jobs God asks us to do, and we will be better able to hear him speaking into our lives.

The way of the cross

You will need two lengths of bramble, and gardening gloves to handle them. If you can get hold of a length of chain as well, this would be excellent; otherwise, rope, or a paper chain will do fine.

Lay the two lengths of bramble to form a cross on the floor, explaining what you are doing for the benefit of those who will not be able to see this. Make the point that you are wearing protective gloves as the brambles are painful. Explain that the brambles represent all the suffering and pain of the cross. Ask for a volunteer to stand at the top end of the cross. This person represents all of us humans, chained up in all the sin and self-ishness that stops us from living freely. (Chain their hands together.) Ask another volunteer to stand at the foot end of the cross, some distance from it. This person represents Jesus.

In Matthew 16:16 we hear how Simon Peter was ready to speak out the truth he had realised about Jesus – that Jesus was the Christ, the Son of the living God. Jesus knew his friends had to be sure of this before they could cope with the next stage of the plan. Now that was in place, and it was time for Jesus to get his friends ready for what had to happen next (see Matthew16:21-25).

Jesus couldn't just go on working in one part of our world, because he had come into the world to save all of us. That would mean walking a very painful road – the way of the cross. The pain of giving his life on the cross was the only way for Jesus to be able to reach us and set us free. He couldn't get round it; he had to go through with it, even though he knew it would hurt.

Ask the person who is representing Jesus to take their shoes off and start walking towards the cross. Before they get there, stop them as you remind people how Simon Peter couldn't bear to think of his friend going through all that pain, and said, 'Never, Lord! This shall not happen to you!' But if Jesus had listened to him (walk round to the representative human in chains), we would never have been set free from the sin that imprisons us. Never. There would have been no hope for us any more.

(Go back to 'Jesus'.) The good and wonderful news is that

Jesus loved us far too much to let his own suffering stop him from saving us. Today we won't make (Lawrence) walk barefoot over those brambles, but as we think of Jesus gladly stepping out to Jerusalem, where he knew he would meet terrible pain and suffering, let's thank him in our hearts for loving us so much that he was prepared to do it anyway (walk round to the human in chains) so that we could all be set free. (Set the person free.)

Mary and Martha

Beforehand make a pair of large card ears, about 30 centimetres high, and a pair of large card hands, about the same size.

Start by asking for two volunteers, one of whom holds the ears to the side of her head, and the other who has the hands fixed to her own hands with large rubber bands. Remind everyone of the two people in Luke 10:38-42, both very good friends of Jesus. Their names were Martha and Mary and they were sisters. Jesus often went round to the home where they lived with their brother Lazarus, and they all enjoyed one another's company.

(Alice) is like a cartoon picture of Mary, because what she liked to do was sit and listen to Jesus and she could listen to him for hours. She probably liked listening to all sorts of people, and may have been the kind of person people could talk easily to because they could see she was interested in them. Mary's idea of cooking a meal was probably beans on toast, and she probably didn't notice the dust creeping up until she could write in it.

(Laura) is like a cartoon picture of Martha, because what she liked best was doing things for people and making sure they had clean shirts and well-balanced meals. Her idea of cooking a meal would be something like roast chicken with all the trimmings. If you wanted something done, you'd ask Martha.

Now people sometimes get upset by this story because they think Jesus is saying that everyone ought to spend their time listening like Mary, and that busy, practical people like Martha aren't somehow as good. But, of course, Jesus isn't saying that at all. His own life was full of work and activity, travelling, preaching, teaching and healing, and none of that would have got done if he hadn't been a doer.

But he also spent hours late at night, or early in the morning on his own with God, talking things over and quietly listening. And he knew that this was a really important part of the doing. He knew we need to keep the right balance between input (the ears) and output (the hands). On that particular visit to Martha and Mary's house, the listening was more important than the doing. What we all have to do is notice when we need to listen, and be ready to stop what we're doing and listen.

All of us need to set aside a quiet time to be with God morning and night, every day. It doesn't have to be long, but it has to be there. If we neglect that, our ability to discern right behaviour will start to slip, and we risk sliding into the kind of life that hurts God so much. Spending time quietly with God is not an optional extra for people with time on their hands, it's an absolute necessity, as well as being refreshing, rejuvenating and problem solving!

Serving two masters

You will need to prepare this talk with another adult. The two of you will be bosses, standing at either end of the church.

Begin by asking for a volunteer who doesn't mind doing a few jobs. This person stands halfway down the church, and you introduce them to the two bosses they are to work for this morning. They are to serve both people as well as they can.

First one boss gives an order, such as to put three chairs out in a line in the middle of the church. As soon as this is done, the other boss gets annoyed that the chairs are arranged like this and tells the servant to put only two chairs out, facing different ways. The first boss tells the servant to put a hymn book on each chair. The other boss tells the servant to put the hymn books away and put a Bible on each chair. Continue the orders so that the poor servant is running about the church pleasing no one.

Thank the volunteer, and explain how Jesus said in Matthew 6:24 that it is impossible to serve two bosses like that. Either you end up loving the first and hating the second, or hating the first and loving the second. It is the same with trying to serve God while we are still bound up with materialism, money and possessions. (Have two signs: 'God' and 'Worldly Riches'. These can include appropriate symbols, such as a cross and some money.) It simply can't be done. While God is whispering to your conscience to live simply and generously, Worldly Riches is insisting that you get the latest fashion in clothes or music. While God is expecting you to commit time to prayer and Bible reading, Worldly Riches is expecting you to commit that time to reading the latest magazines and watching the latest videos.

If we choose to serve God (display the 'God' sign) we have to choose not to serve Worldly Riches. (Tear up the 'Worldly Riches' sign.)

THE GOOD LIFE

For good or evil?

Bring along a kitchen knife, a pen or pencil, a can of paint spray and a £10 or £20 note. You will also need two signs, one saying 'Good' and the other 'Evil'.

Begin by observing that lots of things we handle every day can be used either for good or for evil. Ask for two volunteers to hold the signs, some distance apart, and go through each of the objects in turn, gathering from different people how each can be used. Take the objects to the appropriate notice for each suggestion.

Now ask a person to stand up. It's not only *things* which can be used for good or for evil; it's people as well. Stand the person beside the 'Evil' sign. In what ways can a person use themselves for evil? (Collect suggestions from people of all ages.) Stand the person by the 'Good' sign. In what ways can a person use themselves for good? (Collect suggestions.)

In James 3:9 we read about the tongue: 'We use it to give thanks to our Lord and Father and also to curse our fellow-man, who is created in the likeness of God.' We need to try and use our voices to encourage one another and help one another. We need to use our voices to tell out the truth, and not use the voices God has given to spread unkind gossip, or lies, or to be rude and unkind.

In Romans 6:15-19 St Paul tells us that all the different parts of our bodies can either be offered to sin as instruments of evil, or offered to God as instruments of good. We've looked at our voices. What about our hands? Our minds? Our maleness or our femaleness? Our feet? Our ears? Suggest that during this week they make a point of checking how they are using all the parts of their body, and seeing if they offer all those parts of themselves to God for good.

Dead and alive

In Romans 6:1-11 St Paul tells us that we are to think of ourselves as dead to sin and alive to God through Christ Jesus. What does that mean?

Well, perhaps a few sleeping lions can help. Ask for a few volunteers to play 'sleeping lions' in the aisle, while you and some others try to get them to move. They have to remain as still as they possibly can. Point out that they have to think of themselves as 'asleep' to all those temptations to move which are going on around them. That is rather like us thinking of ourselves being dead to sin. We have to remind ourselves that sin is something which no longer concerns us or has any hold on us.

Ask a few people to say what noises there are in their home at night – any creaks or tickings or chimes. Then draw people's attention to the way we have no difficulty sleeping through these noises, because we know we don't have to worry about them. Some parents will have found that if it isn't your turn to get up and feed the baby you're quite likely to sleep through the crying. You are 'dead' to that sound because you know it isn't anything to do with you. And we are told that we are to think of ourselves as dead to sin.

But it isn't just being dead to sin – it's also being alive to God. What does that mean? Perhaps some people who like chocolate can help us here. Choose a few volunteers and tell them to stand with their backs to you and the congregation. When they think they can detect the presence of chocolate, tell them to raise their hand. Now, as you talk about the way we can always hear what we want to hear, start to open a bar of chocolate, and even though there isn't much sound, and they have their backs to you, it probably won't be very long before they notice, either by hearing or smelling, or both.

That's like us being 'alive' to God. We are going to live as dead to sin, but expectant and interested as far as God is concerned. We will be so tuned in to God that we notice his still, small voice, recognise him in all we see and in those we meet, and live with our hearts and ears and wills turned in his direction all through every day, whatever is going on around us.

Making good

Beforehand arrange for a local builder/decorator to be interviewed, preferably in working clothes and carrying his tools.

Introduce the guest, and ask his advice about a structural problem (either real or imagined). When the builder talks about the importance of all the 'making good', suggest that surely he could just smear some more plaster over the top, and wouldn't that be as good? Or put on thick wallpaper to hide the cracks? Let the builder explain what will eventually happen if the real problem isn't sorted out.

Thank the guest builder and have a couple of the children bring him a mug of tea as it's time for his tea break.

While the builder drinks his tea, explain how what is true for walls and windows is true for us as well. If we have been mean or a pain, or lazy, or if we've been telling lies or living lies, or if there is anything at all in the way we behave which is not right, loving and honest, then we are like a building with bad cracks and damp. As the builder told us, the only way to put it right is to have the wrong things cleared away, and then be built up soundly again.

God can do that in us if we want. He will help us put our lives right, however bad a state they are in. Tell him you are sorry you tell lies, and want to be more honest. He will help you become an honest person who others can trust. Tell God your sister/father-in-law/colleague winds you up and you hate all the rows and want to be more able to cope. God will help you improve those relationships. Tell God you find it hard to share your toys or your money, and want to be more generous. He will help you do it.

But we can't put anything right until we see that there is a problem. It was only when the damp and cracks were noticed that the builder was called in.

John the Baptist spoke about 'repentance'. That means 'Look at your lives; see those cracks and damp patches; and get them sorted out.'

Freed from the yoke

Out of strong card (or a wooden broom handle) make a demonstration yoke to show, on a brave volunteer, how conquerors used to subdue their captives. When you release the volunteer captive, talk to them about how good it feels to be free of the yoke.

In Isaiah 9:2-5 the prophet speaks about his people being freed from the yoke. At the time, the people he was speaking to were being threatened by another country. It looked as if Assyria might well come and yoke the people up as captives, and take them far away from their own homes and their temple and their country, to live in exile in the country of their conquerors.

Isaiah showed the people that if they went on turning away from him by treating the poor unfairly, and spoiling themselves while others starved, then God would not save them from this attack. They were already 'yoked' up as slaves to their greed and selfishness, and their worries about the Assyrians.

Through Isaiah the prophet, God spoke to his people. He told them that he loved them, and that he longed for them to sort their lives out and trust him again. God would then be able to look after them and keep them and their holy city of Jerusalem safe. It would be like their yokes being broken in pieces, so they would be completely free.

Show the demonstration yoke again on another volunteer. Do any of us wear invisible yokes and need to be set free? We may be wearing yokes of selfishness, or resentment; we may be always wishing for things we can't have. We may still feel guilty about something we did. We may need healing of some emotional damage which is holding us back from living freely.

Jesus came so that we could be set free from all these yokes. He's an expert 'yoke shatterer'! He's the kind of light that makes all the darkness in our lives and minds and hearts disappear. If we let him in to walk around our own lives, as well as the lake of Galilee, he will set us free from all those yokes that hold us captive. And then we'll be able to walk through life with a new spring in our step, full of hope.

Taking God's offer

Bring along the details of a children's colouring competition, and also one of those junk mail promotional letters which tell you that you have already been selected as a winner.

Begin by sharing this exciting letter with everyone, reading out some of the blurb, and getting a volunteer to scratch any secret messages included. No doubt many of us receive these kinds of letters. When we do so, we have a choice: are we going to bin it (or preferably recycle it), or will we take them up on their wonderful offer and claim our prize? What we decide will depend on all kinds of factors, such as how busy we are, how desperate for winnings we are, how many previous disappointments we have experienced, and whether we actually believe them.

But one thing is certain. Unless we decide to return our reply slip, we have no chance of winning anything at all. It's the same with colouring competitions. A prize is offered and anyone has a chance of winning. But if you don't get your felt-tips or paints out and do the colouring, and send it off in time, you will have no chance of winning a prize, however good you are at colouring.

Today we are being reminded by God that he has great prizes and gifts for us, which he longs for us to enjoy. He wants to see us all as winners, happily receiving the gift that has been reserved specially for us. But . . . and it is a big 'but' . . . unless we choose to turn to God and take him up on his offer, we will have no chance at all of winning. If we choose wrong instead of right, evil instead of good, and self instead of God, we cannot have the joy and peace and life that God longs to give us. We don't just get it anyway, however we live. Lots of people think that is what happens, but it isn't because God isn't like that. He is a God of goodness and love, truth and kindness. Do we want to go along with that? We have to choose it, then, and start doing something about it.

As soon as we choose it, God can give us all the help we need, and he will, because all he wants is for us to know complete and lasting happiness with him.

The law of love

Hold a large edition of the Bible, and tell everyone that today we are all going to read the whole lot as part of our talk!

Explain that Jesus once gave a summary of the whole of the Bible, in a couple of sentences. (Reader's Digest can eat their heart out!) He was saying that everything in all the law and the prophets was an exploring and working out of this. (Have Matthew 22:37-39 written out large, and invite everyone to join you in reading it out.) There – we've read the Bible! Or, to be more precise, we have read the subject matter of the whole Bible, because everything in it is to do with what we just read – people learning to love God with their whole being, and their neighbours as themselves. It's the story of their learning, their mistakes and failures, and of God's great love helping us make the impossible possible. (Well worth reading the full-length version!)

Let's look at what it means to love others as we love ourselves. How do we love ourselves? Invite a couple of friends to come and help show us. Get one to stand behind the other, with the front person putting their hands behind their back, and the back person providing them with substitute arms by pushing their own arms through the front person's. Have someone offering them a wrapped chocolate which they eat, and give them a brush so they can do their hair.

All day long we look after ourselves like this, feeding and washing and scratching ourselves whenever the needs arise. Even if we don't admit to loving ourselves our actions show that we do. If we start getting too hot, our body kindly makes us sweat to cool us down. If we're threatened by the cold, our helpful body sets us shivering and raises our hairs to warm us up again. And if there's a real emergency (the children can make an ambulance siren sound), the body shuts down some systems and kicks in with others to keep us alive as long as possible. That's love for you!

So if we are to love others like that, we'll be attentive, looking out for one another's well-being and ready to help when we see someone in need. We'll be doing what we can to feed the hungry and look after those with problems. We'll scratch where it itches but not where it doesn't. We'll be ready to drop everything and be there for people if there's an emergency and they need us. We'll do everything we can to help them feel better and get through the difficult times.

And where does all this love come from? From our wonderful God, who made us all in the first place, and loves to see all his children caring for one another like this.

Rules

Talk about some of the rules we are given, such as 'Wear your seatbelt', 'Don't lean out of the window of a moving train', 'Don't play on the railway line' or 'Don't keep poisons in old lemonade bottles'. Gather ideas about why they are good, sensible rules which are worth keeping. Point out that they are good rules whether we actually know the reasons or not.

Now ask for some volunteers to stand around as trees in the garden of the story from Genesis (see Genesis 2:15-17 and 3:1-7). Give the volunteers real or paper fruits to hold. God's rule for Adam and Eve was 'Don't eat fruit from this tree'. Hang this rule round the tree in the centre of the garden. Now God has very good reasons for making this rule, based on his love for Adam and Eve and his concern for them. And since God is God, that rule is the most important thing for Adam and Eve to remember. However tasty the fruit looks, whatever they may be told it will do to help them, they are always to keep hold of God's rule (what was it?), and stick to keeping that. Anything that cuts across God's rule must be wrong.

Ask two people who think they will be able to keep to God's rule without disobeying it. These two are going to be Adam and Eve. Show them how tasty the fruit looks and try to persuade them to try it. Tell them that it will do wonderful things for them, and make them wise like God. When they (hopefully) manage to resist the temptation to do what God's rule told them not to, praise them, and then point out that they managed it this time, but we are always being tempted to be disobedient to God's rule of love, and when it next happens we need to stick close to God, and remember his rule: 'Love God and love one another'.

Adam and Eve in the story stand for all of us who are human. And humans tend not to be very good at resisting temptation. God loves us and understands what it is like to be humans being tempted. We know that because Jesus was tempted during his life on earth. He will give us the strength we need to resist those pressures of temptation, but that doesn't mean it's going to be easy. Resisting temptation is *very hard*, and that's why Jesus told us to pray about it every day of our life: 'Lead us not into temptation but deliver us from evil.' Let's use the strength God offers; we need all the help we can get!

Free to obey

Borrow a toy farm set, or a playmat with animals, houses and cars to arrange on it. Also borrow any remote control vehicle.

Set the youngest children arranging their landscape in a space where they can be seen. Then have the remote control vehicle demonstrated in the aisle. As it is directed to run in different directions, talk about the kind of control the demonstrator has over the vehicle; the vehicle has no choice in the matter. Look at the kind of control demonstrated in the children arranging the animals and buildings. Here, too, they are deciding for the animals what is the best place for them to be. These decisions may be sensitive and based on what the animals would probably like best, but still they have no choice, and must remain in the pond or looking over a fence where they are placed, unless the children decide they need a change.

What about our behaviour in this service? We mostly all sit/stand/kneel in all the right places very obediently, though no one can make us join in attentively if we choose not to, and we could, of course, choose to be very disruptive and spoil it for others.

The Bible tells us that God cared about the people he made. As soon as Adam was made he was invited to help God and share in his work (see Genesis 2:15). God would bring the animals to Adam, and Adam named them (see Genesis 2:18-20). (Take some pictures or animal models to the children and let them name them.) The gardening was not drudgery, but wholesome and rewarding work, with God and people working together.

This is a picture of us all living in harmony with God, obeying him, and living as he suggests is right and good for us. It isn't remote control, with God making us do what he wants. It isn't God doing what is best for us whether we want the best or not. It is God loving us and inviting us to work with him. He lets us choose whether to live this way or not. He hopes we will choose what he knows will make us really deep-down happy, but if we choose ways that mess things up for us or others, he won't stop us. He will just be there ready to dry our tears and help us try again when we realise how foolish we have been.

Living together

Ask for two volunteers of about the same height (or several pairs of volunteers) and tie the ankles of each pair together. They can practise walking three- legged around the church. As they do so, point out how difficult it is until you get the hang of walking in step with one another. This is one of the most important lessons we can learn in life.

We are all given other people to live with. People in our families like brothers and sisters, mums, dads, grandparents, aunts, uncles and cousins. Is it easy, just because we are related? No! Sometimes it's very good fun, like when we're all getting on together and making one another laugh, and listening to what the others are saying, and the others understanding when you come home fed up.

At other times it's very hard living with those close to us. Like when everyone wants something different and no one wants to do the washing-up, and so on. That's a bit like when we get in a tangle of feet in the three-legged race and trip one another up. When we start to think it would be a lot easier to live on our own without other people around.

What Saint Paul suggests is that we need to live in step with one another, learning to do things like forgiving one another, being patient, letting someone else have the best sometimes, co-operating instead of getting at each other's throats all the time (see Colossians 3:12-17). That's the Christian way. That's Jesus' way. It may also mean comforting one another, sharing one another's suffering. It's really learning to love in the way Jesus talked about love.

When we live like this, we and the people we are joined up with, in our families and at school and at work, won't need to keep tripping one another up. We'll be able to live more supportively, enjoying one another as God meant us to.

The right point of view

Begin by drawing attention to the direction everyone is facing in church. Obviously this will vary according to your architecture and the age of the building. The architecture reflects a focus and a general direction which the planners thought of most importance. Perhaps if you were all about to start planning from scratch, you might arrange things slightly differently!

Once you have established the general seating focus, move to another part of the church, such as the entrance. If people are going to continue facing you, they will all have to turn round. That is because at the moment the important thing going on is you speaking, and that takes over in importance from the general focus of the building.

Now move somewhere else so that everyone has to turn round again. In Matthew 5:17-48 Jesus taught about the Law, which is summed up in the ten commandments. Have these displayed on card, or on an OHP, or walk to the part of the church where they are written on the wall. They are good rules to live by and our whole law system is still based on them. But with all rules there is a problem. Jesus wanted his followers (and that includes us) to remember that the really important thing is to stay focused on God in everything we do.

Perhaps you haven't ever killed someone. But the spirit of the law means more than that, just as our focus is more than just sitting facing the front. It also means making sure we haven't got unkind or destructive thoughts about people, that we're not making people feel stupid or useless, that we aren't putting other people down or running them down behind their backs, because those things are in the destructive spirit of hate, which is the opposite of God's law of love. As you mention each of these, move around the building so people have to move their 'attitudes' to see you.

What we need to do is keep our eyes fixed on Jesus, and whatever we are doing we can think to ourselves, 'Does this thing I'm doing or saying or thinking make Jesus happy? Is it a loving thing to do or think or say?'

And if it is, carry on. If it isn't, stop and change direction.

Like salt and light

You will need a large saucepan, a pack of spaghetti, a jar of Italian sauce and a large carton of salt, a jug, a teacup and a tablespoon. You will also need a table lamp and a bright spotlight.

Produce the first set of items, setting them out and talking about cooking pasta. Invite a good cook from the congregation to supervise! Explain that the best cookery books say that pasta can't be seasoned after it's cooked, so we need to add the salt to the cooking water. Pick up the salt, and wonder aloud how much salt to use. A jugful? Get the cook to explain what would happen if you put in that much salt. A teacupful? Still too much! A tablespoonful? Still too much. If we use that much all we will taste will be the salt, and the whole idea of salt is that it isn't really noticed but brings out the flavour of the other ingredients.

That's what we are called to do as Christians (see Matthew 5:13): not to take over and dominate or possess people, or want to control them, but in humility to make ourselves available and useful in helping to give other people the freedom and the confidence to be themselves. That may mean more listening and less speaking; it may mean being less concerned about being thought important and more concerned about other people's needs being recognised. It is the way of quiet, loving service.

Now flash the spotlight around so that it goes in people's eyes (but don't overdo this!). Explain that Jesus also calls us to be light (see Matthew 5:14-16). That doesn't mean trying to blind people with our natural brilliance, or trying subtly to impress others, so that we're more like disco lights, designed for a flashy effect. The kind of light we are called to be is a much more practical sort, rather like a table lamp, perhaps, which simply helps people to see better, so they don't bump into things and hurt themselves, and so they can get on with living more effectively.

Salt and light are just simple things, but they are things which can make a great difference. As Christians we are called to be like that – just our ordinary selves, but through our faith in God, able to make a difference.

Loving our enemies

Beforehand ask the children to make lots of paper chains.

Remind everyone that Jesus teaches us to love our enemies and forgive those who sin against us (see Luke 6:27-36). How on earth are we supposed to do it? Surely enemies are people you hate? Why does Jesus tell us to love them, then?

Ask a volunteer to run and skip around a bit and talk about how life can feel when we are happy with ourselves, and everything is going well for us. But sooner or later we get into a mood with someone, someone upsets us and annoys us, someone else winds us up, someone makes our life a real misery, someone lets us down and spoils our plans, someone hurts a person we love, or someone steals from us a close friend or a marriage partner, or our dignity in old age. (At each suggestion, drape a chain around the volunteer until s/he is smothered in chains.) And if we haven't forgiven these people who have sinned against us and hurt us, we end up still carrying invisible chains which weigh us down. The volunteer can walk around bowed down with the heavy chains.

So when Jesus says to us, 'Love your enemies and forgive those who wrong you', he knows it is hard, but he also knows it will set us free to live fully again. Every time we say (and really mean it) 'I forgive you for what you did', a chain drops off. (Pull a chain off the volunteer.) Every time we wrestle with our feelings of hate for someone and ask God to help us sort things out, a chain drops off. (Pull off another chain.) Pull off the remaining chains, with everyone saying 'I forgive you!' for each one.

Jesus doesn't like to see us weighed down with heavy invisible chains of hate and resentment and bitterness against people. He wants us to be free to enjoy life, and he will always help us to do the forgiving. Forgiving is not easy; it's very hard work. If you know there is someone you are finding it very hard to forgive, ask God for the grace to forgive and then work at the forgiving. Don't live with the chains any more.

Shining

You will need a hand mirror.

Begin by asking everyone if they have noticed how people often look like their pets, particularly dogs! Perhaps they choose a pet which reflects their own character. Today we are looking at how spending our lives with God makes us more and more like him.

Use the mirror to catch the light and throw it on to people's faces. Mirrors are excellent at spreading light around, because they are able to reflect light. Moses, who was a close friend of God was the person who led the people of Israel out of Egypt, where they had been slaves, and through the desert to the promised land. When Moses had been on a mountain in God's company and was given the Ten Commandments, he came down from the mountain with his face glowing and radiant. Like a mirror, he was reflecting some of the glory of God (see Exodus 34:29-35). Sometimes if people are really happy – a bride and bridegroom getting married to the one they love, students hearing they have passed all their exams really well, or children on their birthday – we talk about them looking radiant, or glowing with happiness. How we are feeling and thinking inside changes the way we look.

When Jesus was on earth, three of his close friends were on a mountain with him when he was praying, and they saw him not just with a radiant face, but completely shining, or trans-figured (see Luke 9:28-36). What they were seeing was the glory of God in Jesus, who was and is completely at one with God, his Father. They heard God's voice explaining who Jesus was and telling them to listen to him. Not like listening to music in the background, but really attentive listening, like you would listen to instructions for flying an aeroplane if you were the only person on board able to bring it safely to land.

When we live our lives close to Jesus like this, listening to his quiet voice guiding us, talking over our problems and happiness with him, and working at living a good life, then gradually our faces will start to show some of God's glory, and our lives will start to shine, reflecting God's loving nature like mirrors (flash the light again) reflecting the light.

Tasters of heaven

Bring along some tasters of a particular cheese, tiny chunks such as those you find in most supermarkets from time to time. Bring also a block of the same cheese, labelled.

Show your tray of tasters for the cheese you have brought to recommend. Suggest that people try a taster of it to see whether they like it. Since these tasters came off the main block of cheese, you can guarantee that they will taste as good as the main block. Discuss their findings briefly.

Although we haven't been to heaven, God gives us lots of little 'tasters' which help us find out what it is like. Whenever we sense Jesus giving us peace of mind or joy, or the lovely knowledge that God really loves and cares for us, we are getting a taster of life after death. Jesus lives in heaven so when he comes into us, he doesn't leave heaven behind but brings it with him. So the more we live in God's company and follow Jesus, the more of heaven we will have in our lives even before we die.

Explain that lots of people think Christians are crazy believing that there is life after death. Since they can't see beyond death, they don't think there can be anything like heaven. If I had never seen the yellow daffodil flowers in spring, I would probably think people were crazy burying dry bulbs in their earth at this time of year. But because I have seen what happens to those bulbs, I trust that they won't just rot in the ground. If I were a caterpillar, I would probably laugh at anyone suggesting that one day I would be flying about with colourful wings. It isn't true that the only real things are those we can see.

It is sometimes difficult to trust that what we can't see is still there, but we make the effort to do it whenever we drive in fog, walk along looking around instead of at the path under our feet, or wash our backs. So it is quite possible. And Jesus has told us that there really is life after death, and lots of people saw him alive after he had died. So we aren't crazy for believing there is life after death; we happen to know it's true, and we've already tasted little bits of how lovely it is.

FAITH

Seeing the invisible

You will need a hairdrier or a fan, or a lit candle to blow out.

Start with a riddle. You're thinking of something which is all around us, pressing against our faces and bodies at 15 pounds per square inch. It goes in and out of us all the time we're alive, and there's lots of it right in front of our eyes. What is it? (Air.) But we can't see it, so how do we know it's there?

Put on the hairdrier or fan, or ask someone to blow the candle out. When air moves, we can see what it does. When we try to hold our breath we realise how much our bodies need air to live.

God is here as well, and we can't see him. No one has ever seen God while they are alive on earth. So how can God tell us what he is like, when we can't see him?

There are ways we can see what God is like by what he does and by what he creates. If we look at the world we can see that God must be generous, imaginative, careful, clever, organised, hopeful and happy to let us work with him.

But God had an even better idea. If he could walk among humans as a human, then all the humans who lived at the time or at any time afterwards would be able to see exactly how God behaves. We could see it in our own human language. The language of doing, thinking, feeling and speaking.

In John 1:1-18 Jesus is talked about as being the Word, or the Message of God. When we look at how Jesus lived and died, we are looking straight at God, even though we can't see God with our eyes.

And what do we see? John describes Jesus as being 'full of grace and truth'. Have this written up on a sheet. Around it you can add other people's ideas. Head the page 'Jesus is' and display it for the rest of the service.

Growing in faith

Beforehand ask a family to help you by providing a couple of clothing items which are now too small for their child to wear. Or you could borrow a cub/brownie sweater which once you would have been able to get into. Also find a sprouting acorn, or a similar example of life bursting out of confines.

Begin by talking about the way we grow out of our clothes. Sometimes we like a sweater or jacket so much that we want to go on wearing it even when it's a bit short or tight, but eventually we realise that we just can't get into it any more, and we'll have to hand it down to someone younger or smaller. As you talk about this, use the children and their skimpy clothes to illustrate how silly it looks and how uncomfortable it feels to wear something which is much too small for us, and then try the same garment on someone it fits to see the difference.

Remind everyone that we are spiritual as well as physical, and we can grow out of things spiritually as well. Some of the early Christians thought that it wasn't right for non-Jewish people to be allowed to join the Church. In Acts 11:1-18 Peter realised that was like wearing a sweater which was too small, and God's ideas were much bigger than they had thought. He wanted everyone to be part of his love, with no one left out. So the early church very sensibly took off that outgrown idea.

When we are very young, we are taught to pray prayers we can understand. That's wonderful. But if we are still praying like a three-year-old when we are thirteen or twenty-three, or fifty-three, we are wearing skimpy spiritual clothes that we have really outgrown. Unless we realise that, and take them off, and find ways of praying that fit, we won't be able to move forward where God wants us to go.

Take a look at the acorn. Acorns are lovely to hold and play with, just as they are. But the oak tree can't become its huge, leafy self unless it breaks out of the acorn, and leaves that behind.

Jesus gives us all a rule, or command. We are to love one another. As soon as we start this kind of responsible, caring love for one another, we are bound to start growing. Sometimes the growing hurts. Sometimes the growing feels exciting. Sometimes the growing is hard work. And always the growing will be breaking out of where we were before. This means that, like children growing taller year by year, we will not be able to keep wearing the same old spiritual clothes. God won't let us get set in our ways because he goes on having exciting plans for us right through our lives, no matter how old we get.

Seeing and believing

Beforehand place a tape or CD in your pocket. Begin by telling everyone that you have got an orchestra in your pocket and asking them if they believe you. Then show them the tape or CD. Now they have seen with their eyes they know exactly what was in your pocket. And now that they understand what it is, they can see that you were right – you did have an orchestra in your pocket, but not in the way they expected!

Jesus had told his friends that he would have to suffer and die before rising to new life, and they hadn't understood what he meant. Even when Jesus was dying, nailed to the cross, they didn't realise that this had to happen if we were to be saved from sin and death. Instead they felt miserable and let down and lost and confused. They didn't believe because they hadn't seen for themselves. (Put the tape back in your pocket.)

Then, on the first Easter evening, Jesus was suddenly there with them. He was alive, talking with them and they were so excited and overjoyed to have him there again. Now that they had seen him they knew it was true that he was alive (see John 20:19-29). (As you say this bring out the tape from your pocket again, but don't refer to it. It will simply help them make connections.)

But it was also different from what they might have thought. Jesus wasn't exactly the same as before. With this new life he was able to be there without having unlocked the doors. He could appear and disappear. But he was a real person, not a ghost. He didn't make the disciples feel scared; he filled them with peace and happiness.

At last they began to understand what he had meant when he had talked to them about dying and rising again. They began to understand that God's love had to go right through death, loving and forgiving the whole way, so as to win the battle against evil. When Jesus came through death and out into the light of new life, he was like a butterfly coming out of its chrysalis – the same but completely different, free and beautiful.

Thomas and the others needed to see Jesus with their eyes for quite a few times after the Resurrection. They now had to learn that he was always there with them, even if they couldn't see him.

Don't worry

Beforehand prepare some large speech bubbles from thin card, with the typical worries of those in the congregation written clearly on them. Here are some suggestions:

- My hair's going grey/thin on top!
- What can I wear?
- Weetabix or cocopops or toast?
- Suppose they don't like me?
- Brut or Denim – and how much of it?
- I'm the wrong shape!

Ask some volunteers to hold these worries up high. They're the kind of things we all waste our time and energy worrying about. Jesus was sad to see people worrying their lives away, and he wanted them to be free of this constant worrying. Point out that the volunteers will start to get aching arms if they have to go on holding the worries up for too long.

Matthew tells us that Jesus says to us, 'Put all those worries down – they're heavy to carry and are making your arms ache.' (See Matthew 6:25-34) Let the volunteers put the worries down, and talk about what a relief it is to have our worries sorted out.

Jesus wants us to know that although life is bound to be full of difficult and uncomfortable times as well as easy and happy times, we don't need to worry about it as well as live through it! That makes it twice as bad for us. The way to be free of worry is not to be massively rich or refuse to grow up, or bury your head in the sand and pretend not to see the problems. The way to be free of worrying yourself sick is to trust that your Parent God loves you, likes you, and is well able to help you cope with everything you'll face in your life.

Jesus suggests we live one day at a time, instead of worrying about things that might never happen, or which are bound to happen, and God will bring us safely through it all to heaven, where we will be safe with God for ever.

Learning to trust

Ask for one volunteer who is brave and one who is more scared and timid. Tell the timid one that you are asking them to fall backwards. You promise them they won't come to any harm (but you don't say you will catch them). Suggest that they watch the brave volunteer to try it first, so they can see what happens. Now ask the brave volunteer to fall backwards, and make sure you catch them, or arrange to have someone strong to catch them.

Now ask if the timid person is able to try it, now that they have seen that it is safe. If they are, let them try it, making certain they are safely caught!

Sometimes it is very hard to know whether we can trust something or not unless we have seen it in action. Perhaps we have bought a tape recorder, or a jigsaw puzzle at a boot sale or a jumble sale, and it looks fine, and we are assured that it's in good working order. But when we get home we find the tape recorder chews up our favourite tape, and the jigsaw puzzle has two or three pieces missing.

It's all very disappointing to be let down like that. And the longer we live, and the more we are let down by things or by people, the more disappointed we get, and the more determined we are not to trust anyone or anything in case we are let down again. Thomas was a bit like that. He had probably been badly let down by people during his life. Like lots of us, it made him scared to trust good news. We and Thomas would love good news to be true, but we'd rather not trust it at all than trust it and risk being let down.

Now Jesus himself knows that he is alive, and will stay alive for ever. He knows it would be quite safe for us to believe this, because he knows it's true! He hopes very much that we will be able to believe, because he knows it will make such a wonderful difference to our lives – we'll be able to live in a new kind of freedom, and become more and more our real selves.

So what does he do about it? In John 20:19-29 we hear how Jesus came into the room, joining his friends as they were praying, so that they knew he was there. And Jesus still does that, nearly two thousand years later. He is here now, with us, his friends. Whenever we gather in Jesus' name, he joins us.

When we live on the lookout for him, we'll find we start noticing him more and more. We won't see him with our eyes, but we'll feel his love and peace, and suddenly know he is there.

Go for it!

Beforehand collect some 'special offers' from your junk mail during the week and from local shops. Also make one sign that says, 'Not today, thanks!' and another that says, 'Yes, I'll go for it!' Ask everyone (or just the children) to shout out the words on the signs whenever you show them.

Start by talking about the special offers in your collection, referring to those which people of different ages in the congregation might find interesting, amusing and completely ridiculous. Ask a volunteer to display the general view of people about various offers by holding up the appropriate sign. Point out that in all these special offers we are free to choose whether to take advantage of the offer or not, and if it's something we really want and like we're likely to say, 'Yes, I'll go for it!' If we don't think we need the item on offer then we don't think it's worth having and we're more likely to say, 'Not today, thanks!'

Jesus' special offer to us is extremely good value. He offers to make himself at home in our lives and set us free from all the things that imprison us, so that we can really live to the full, not just now, but after death as well. For ever, in fact. How much does it cost? Nothing. Or rather, everything, but Jesus has already paid the complete cost for us.

As it's such a good offer you'd think that everyone would rush to take him up on it. (Display the 'Yes, I'll go for it!' sign.) But Luke 13:34 tells us that there have always been lots of people who have refused the offer and turned it down. (Display the 'Not today, thanks!' sign.) In this verse we see Jesus really sad. What has made him so sad is that he has been longing to give people the love he knows they need and yet they won't let him give them this free gift which could make their whole lives rich.

Perhaps we don't think we need God's love and help. Perhaps we are afraid to accept because it seems just too good to be true. Perhaps we think it can't be possible because we don't think we're worth something as good as this. Whatever the reasons, lots of us humans end up saying 'Not today, thanks!' to the best special offer ever. That means losing out on all the good things God is hoping to give us during our lives on earth and our lives in heaven. Things like joy and peace of mind, contentment and fulfilment, a sense of really being alive and living life the best way there is.

Abram was a 'Yes, I'll go for it!' person. He took God up on his offer and believed God would put his action where his mouth was. As a result his life was greatly blessed. And God did keep his promise to make Abram's descendants as many as the uncountable stars in the sky.

God will never force us to say 'Yes, I'll go for it!' when we really want to say 'Not today, thanks!' But before anyone says 'Not today, thanks!' to God's special offer of his freely given love, they would be wise to think it over very carefully. It's such a fantastic offer that the only wise thing to say is, 'Yes, I'll go for it!'

Fashion or faith?

Beforehand gather a selection of brand-name items relevant to each age group in the congregation.

Begin by displaying each item and drawing attention to the brand name to impress people. Talk about how we are sometimes made to feel we have to have a particular thing in order to be thought normal or worth anything. Sometimes we are teased if we haven't got them. Sometimes we go out shopping to cheer ourselves up, thinking that having more will make us happy. Sometimes we spend money we can't afford to keep up with our friends or neighbours.

Put all the items into a carton labelled 'Very Important' and close the lid. Explain that Jesus turns our ideas of what is important upside down. As you say this, turn the carton upside down. Jesus told people that trust in what you can buy and possess is not the good thing the advertisements say it is, and these things don't give us long-term happiness at all (see Luke 12:15-34).

So what does he offer instead?

Jesus says that we will be much happier if we trust in God rather than in things people say about us, and things people make and sell. Getting stuck in the 'wanting something else' mode or the 'everybody else does it' mode just ends up making us dissatisfied and greedy and selfish, which doesn't bring happiness to us or those we live with. But if we put our trust in God, all the riches of the kingdom of God will be ours. We'll enjoy the lovely and surprising ways God provides for our needs. We'll be able to see what is good and right, and want to work enthusiastically again instead of just going through the motions. We won't be frantically running to keep up with the latest fashion. We won't be so anxious about material things.

Jesus doesn't say we'll have lots of comforts or fame or money if we live like this. In fact he says we will run into insults and people will think we're crazy, and they will laugh at us and make life difficult for us. We can't say we haven't been warned!

But the rewards far outweigh the disadvantages. Putting our trust in God will enable us to live as free, contented and generous-hearted people – the kind of people we would, deep down, probably prefer to be.

Walking by faith

You will need a pair of swimming flippers. Have ready a couple of large freezer labels with the words 'I believe in God' written on them.

Ask for a volunteer to walk up and down the church, so that everyone can see the way this person normally walks. Now give them the flippers to wear. As they are being put on, explain how our faith in God affects the way we live. Remind them of Abraham and the way he was ready to get up and go when God asked him to, even though he didn't know exactly how the move would work out. He trusted God to want the best for him, and had faith that God would look after him (see Hebrews 11:8-12).

Now that the volunteer is wearing flippers, is he going to walk in the same way as before? Well, let's see. As the person walks up and down, point out that we can all see the effect the flippers are having on the walking – it's a very distinctive flipper walk!

Put the freezer labels on the flippers, explaining that when we decide to walk with faith in God, that is going to affect the way we walk through life. It will give us a very distinctive faith walk. We will be stopping doing what is wrong and learning to do what is right. We will be noticing the needs of those around us and in our world, and making sure we help out with our time and prayers and money. We will be building up treasure in heaven by our loving kindness, patience, honesty, thoughtfulness and self-control.

The wisdom of faithfulness

Today is a good opportunity to celebrate the elderly faithful and build relationships between young and old. Beforehand arrange for an elderly man and woman to sit at the front with a microphone to answer a few questions put to them by the children about what life was like when they were children. Gather the children round their feet and introduce the elderly people. Since they have been alive a long time they have picked up lots of wisdom. They have lived through things the younger ones here have heard about in history. Invite the children to find out what it was like being a child 70 or more years ago – they can ask about clothes, toys, school, church or food, for instance. After a few questions thank the volunteers and have the children escort them back to their seats.

When Jesus was a baby, Joseph and Mary brought him into the temple (see Luke 2:22-38). All Jewish families did this when their first son was born. They came to give a present, or offer a sacrifice to God and dedicate the child. We've had two wise, elderly people answering questions today. And when Mary, Joseph and Jesus came into the temple there were two wise elderly people there. Their names were Simeon and Anna. They had both loved God all their life, and if any of us do that, we will end up wise and lovable in our old age. You can't love God all your life and end up crabby and narrow-minded.

Jesus didn't have a big label tied round his swaddling clothes saying 'I am the Messiah'. Joseph and Mary didn't wave flags or shout to everyone, 'Look! This is the baby you've all been waiting for!' From the outside he looked just like any other baby, and Mary and Joseph looked just like an ordinary, fairly poor set of parents, rather dusty after the journey.

So how did Simeon and Anna know that this baby was the one they were waiting for?

Simeon had been told that he would see the promised Messiah in person before he died. He had been listening to God all his life, and because he was used to listening to God, he was able to recognise that this particular baby was the Messiah, God's chosen one.

When we spend a lot of time with another person we get to know how they think, and we understand them better and better. If we spend time with God every day, starting from today, and carry on doing that right into our old age, we will get to know him better and better, and it won't be long before we are able to hear what he speaks into our hearts. It is astounding that the powerful creator of this universe is happy to communicate with individuals like this, but that's God for you. He's hoping there will be some wise and faithful elderly Christians in the future – twenty, thirty, forty, fifty, sixty, seventy or eighty years from now. There could be. It could be us.

PARABLES

Seeds and soil

You will need a seed tray filled with seed compost, some large-sized seeds, a dibber (to poke holes for the seeds) and a cloth bag of pearl barley. You will also need to arrange for a broom to sweep up the scattered barley after the talk. Lay down in the aisle one large piece of paper to represent a rocky patch, and a few footsteps to represent a stony path.

You might like to play a snatch of the *Gardeners' World* theme tune at the beginning, as you set out the seed tray and compost on a table and invite a couple of keen gardeners in the congregation to demonstrate planting. As the gardeners work, talk with them about why the seed planted like this is more likely to be successful than if we just shake the seeds outside.

In Matthew 13:1-9 Jesus told a parable which was all about seeds being sown, and the best growing conditions. Of course, it wasn't just about seeds being planted and growing. Parables are stories with secrets inside, and the secret of this story is that it was really all about us, and how we respond to God's word when we hear it. This is how it works.

Where Jesus lived, it was very rocky, and the farmers had fields with bare rock showing here and there (put down the paper), and stony roads that went right through the middle (put down the footprints). They ploughed the earth in long furrows, like we did here in the seed tray, only much bigger of course, and then the person sowing the seed walked up and down the furrows sowing the seed like this. (Demonstrate with your bag of pearl barley, scattering the seed to left and right.) The problem is that not all the seed goes in the nice soil you have prepared. When God's word is spoken, we are not always ready to accept it. Let's look at where some of those seeds have landed.

Involve a volunteer to look at the stony path and stand over any seeds they find there. Sometimes we read or hear God's teaching and we're more like a stony path than good soil. It just goes in one ear and out of the other, and we hardly notice what we've heard. We might sit here for the readings and our thoughts fly in, like birds, and take away God's message so we don't even remember what was said.

What about the rocky ground? (Send a volunteer there.) Sometimes we hear God's message and get really keen, and take on far too much far too early, so, like plants growing up on rocky soil, we haven't got good roots. We burn ourselves out and drop away.

What about the soil next to the rock? (Send a volunteer there.) Lots of weeds grow here, so there's a lot of competition for the seeds. Sometimes we hear God's message, but there are so many other things going on in our lives, which we consider important, that the really important message of God gets choked and crowded out.

But all the rest is in good soil. We are like good soil when we listen to God's teaching carefully, think about it and what it means, and then live with it. That way we shall certainly grow and produce a good harvest. Let's check this week that we are taking good notice of God's words to us, and giving him proper space and time, so that we grow in his love.

Lost sheep

Gather a mixed group of 'sheep', and appoint a shepherd who is given a crook. Talk about the way the shepherd looks after sheep, finding fresh water and fresh grass, and protecting them from the dangers of wolves and bears. Sometimes a sheep will wander off on its own. (Send one of the sheep to go off and hide somewhere in the church, ensuring that enthusiastic sheep are prevented from going right outside.)

Jesus thought the way we wander off from living good lives was rather like sheep wandering off and getting lost. He loves all of us, and doesn't want any of us to be lost, so, like a good shepherd, he checks that all the rest of the people in the church are OK. (Are they?) Then he sets off to search for the one who has wandered off (see Luke 15:4-7).

As the shepherd searches for the lost sheep (tell him/her to wait with the sheep when it is found), give some examples of what makes us wander off from God. Perhaps other things crowd God out and take over our life; perhaps we want to disobey God's rules and please ourselves; perhaps some tragedy in our life shakes our faith, and we think God has caused the pain instead of realising that he is weeping with us. Whatever it is, once we realise we are a long way from God, we feel very lost and alone. Sometimes we have got ourselves trapped in habits we can't break out of on our own.

Thankfully Jesus, our good shepherd, is out looking for us, and he will search and search until he finds us. We can help by bleating – which is praying, calling out to God from where we are.

It is very good to be found. As the shepherd brings the wandering sheep, hand in hand, back to the flock, talk about how wonderful it is to know that we are forgiven, and that God loves us enough to forgive us even when we ran away from him. When the sheep comes back to the flock everyone can clap, as, with all the angels of heaven, we celebrate the truth that our God is such an excellent rescuer, full of understanding and mercy, and willing to give up his life to get us back home again.

Wheat and weeds

Borrow and bring along one of those toys (Polly Pocket or Mighty Max) which look like a plain box and hold inside a whole miniature world.

Show everyone the toy, and explain that today we're going to look at another of those parables which Jesus told. Parables are a bit like these toys, because they are stories which have secret meanings inside. You need to open up the story to find the meaning. (Open the toy.) First of all, let's look at the story Jesus told (see Matthew 13:24-30).

If you have an OHP you can illustrate the story using cut-outs of weeds and wheat, and the evil enemy based on the pictures below, as these will show up in silhouette on the screen.

Remind everyone of the story, using volunteers to be the farmer sowing his seed (accompanied by music from *The Archers*), and the evil enemy creeping into the field at night to sow the weeds (accompanied by everyone doing a pantomime hiss). When the farmer finds that his field is sprouting loads of weeds as well as wheat, he is faced with a choice (hold a question mark in a thought bubble over his head).

All the servants say, 'Shall we pull the weeds out for you?' (Have this written on a speech bubble so everyone, or a small group, can say it together.)

The farmer shakes his head. (He does.) He knows that if he pulls all the weeds up now he might pull out some of the wheat as well, and he certainly doesn't want to lose any of his wheat. So instead he decides to let both the wheat and the weeds grow together until harvest time, when the weeds can be gathered up and burnt, and the wheat harvested and put in the barn.

That's the parable Jesus told. What's the secret meaning of it?

Here's a clue. The field is the world, and we can all see that in our world there is a lot of good, but also a lot of evil. Why doesn't God burst out of heaven and stop all the evil in the world straightaway, and punish the people who get away with doing cruel and terrible things?

The parable gives us the answer.

If he did that while life is still going on – while the wheat and weeds are still growing – some good might get lost or damaged. It is because God cares about us so much that he won't risk anything that would cause us lasting harm. There's time enough for punishment when the world comes to an end. Then all that is good and honest and kind and thoughtful will be gathered up safely for ever. All that is mean and selfish, cruel and greedy will be completely destroyed for ever. We can trust our God to know the right time to punish and the right time to hold back, because he always acts with love and mercy as well as justice.

Real goodness

Bring with you an egg cup, a whole egg in its shell, and a boiled egg which someone has eaten, so that just the shell is left, with a spoon hole at one end. Put this into the egg cup upside down so that it looks like a complete egg ready to eat. You will also need an egg spoon.

Begin by talking about those times you've desperately needed help, like missing the bus when you're already a bit late, or being caught in a downpour on your way to school, and you're hoping one of your friends will happen to drive past and see you. Perhaps the man who had been mugged in Jesus' story about the good Samaritan (see Luke 10:25-37) felt a bit like that, if he was still able to think after the beating-up he'd been given. Perhaps in the daze of his injuries he heard each set of footsteps coming nearer, and hoped that now he'd get some help. But no, the footsteps quickened up when they got nearer and then went off into the distance again. And the man still lay there, unable to move.

Perhaps he had almost given up hope when the Samaritan, a foreigner, stopped and came to peer at him to see what was wrong. Perhaps, as he swayed in and out of consciousness, he was half aware of being carefully given first aid, of being comforted and reassured that he was going to be all right. Those are good things to feel and hear, when you're in great need. You have no power at such times to make anyone care for you, so all you can do is rely on other people choosing to treat you well.

And that's what we're being taught today: that as Christians we are people called to treat others well, whether we're told to or not, whether anyone sees us or not, whether we want to or not. Why? Simply because our God says that this is the right and good way to live.

And the man in the Gospel, to whom Jesus told his 'good neighbour' story, could recite the rules he was supposed to live by off by heart: 'Love the Lord your God with all your heart and with all your soul and with all your strength and with all your mind. And love your neighbour as yourself.' But for him and for lots of others, those words are like this boiled egg. It looks wonderful and full of goodness. But if I start to dig into it (do that) with my spoon, I find that all the inside is missing, and there's nothing of any goodness there at all.

We must be brave and dig into the words we sing and pray together today, and look at what we find inside. Perhaps there will be rich meaning, and you will know that the words your mouth says are backed up with the way you live. Perhaps you will find the words are just a shell, and your life doesn't back them up at all. If so, come to God today and ask him to fill the shell with new meaning. He can do that, and he's waiting for you to ask.

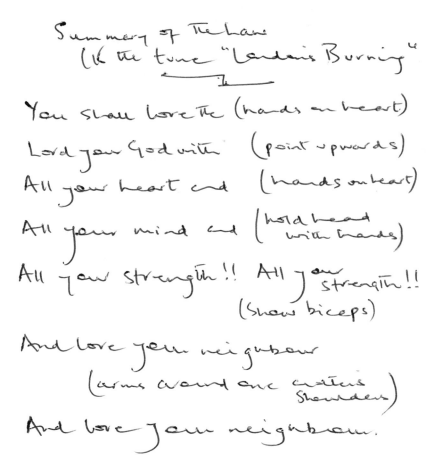

Comfort or concern?

Arrange for the following items to be in church today, giving different people responsibility for them, so that they will emerge from various people all over the congregation: a pair of sunglasses, some well-known expensive brand of sun cream (the bottle can be empty), a luxurious, squashy cushion, a bottle of champagne (or a champagne bottle) in an ice bucket, and a tape/ CD player with some easy-listening music in it ready to play. At the front of the church you need one of those comfortable sun-loungers. Arrange for another person to walk quietly to the middle of the aisle with a begging bowl and sit down there.

Get the sun-lounger out and invite someone to be cosseted and pampered for a few minutes of the morning. They can lie on the lounger, and various people from all over the church bring them all their comforts. Enthuse about each item as you make the volunteer really comfortable. Leave them snoozing in luxury as you pose the question: 'Is there anything wrong with living in wealth and luxury, and pampering ourselves?'

In itself, no, there isn't. Of course it is good to have times of rest and relaxation, and it is fine to enjoy the good things of life. But if we use wealth to cushion ourselves from the real world, shield our eyes from the harsh glare of suffering, protect ourselves from feeling people's pain, block out the sound of people's crying, and deaden our sense of duty, then we run the danger of rejecting all the needs, and not feeling we have any responsibility to do anything about them anyway. (Hold a 'speech bubble' of card over the volunteer, which says, 'What problems?')

In Jesus' story about the rich man and Lazarus (see Luke 16:19f), the rich man was probably a nice guy, and there is no mention of him doing anything really evil. But he simply hadn't noticed the beggar who sat at his own front gate every day. Point out that all the time we've been enjoying indulging ourselves up here, there has been someone begging down there.

It's all too easy for us to ignore the needs. Jesus reminds us to check that our lack of poverty doesn't prevent us from doing the practical caring love we are called to.

True wealth

You will need the packing boxes for various consumables, such as a computer, electronic game, microwave, brand-name shoes, or luxury biscuits. You will also need such things as a CD, gardening and teenage magazines, and a film carton. Choose the items to suit the interests of the people in your congregation, and have enough for one person to hold all at once with great difficulty. Finally, you need a pocket Bible and a tiny spray of flowers.

Remind everyone of the story Jesus told in Luke 12:13-21, about the farmer who thought that having a bumper harvest, and therefore a financial windfall, meant total security, so that he could just do as he liked and take no care of his soul. His greed had made him foolish. As it happened, he was going to die and face God that very night, and he wasn't in the least prepared for death.

Ask for a volunteer to help you explain something. Explain how all the advertisements tell us that if we get a particular brand of yoghurt or car or shampoo, everyone will like us and fancy us, and we'll be really happy. Sometimes we get taken in by this lie, and start wanting to have things so we'll be safer or happier or better liked.

Go through the things we like to get, piling the packages into the arms of the volunteer as you talk. When they are completely loaded up, and have no hands left to hold anything else, point out the problem with all this 'having' being important to us. It means that when Jesus offers us his Word and his Love (offer the Bible and flowers), we simply haven't room to take it, and we turn it down, because our minds are too full of what we've got and what we want, and how we're going to hang on to what we've got.

And that is a tragedy that lasts not just for a few years but for ever. We need to put down our wanting and having, so that we can take the really important wealth that God offers us. (The volunteer is helped to unload, so they can hold the Bible and flowers.) These are the things which will make us content and happy and secure, whether we have all the other good things or not.

Treasures old and new

Bring along something that is precious and old, and something that is precious and new. Choose items which your congregation are likely to relate to. (It could be a well-worn teddy and a new Teletubby for a baby, for instance, or an old stained-glass window in the church and someone's new engagement ring.)

First introduce everyone to the old thing, pointing out why it is so treasured and important and valuable. In our faith there are also ancient things which we as Christians value and treasure, such as the stories in the Old Testament which teach us about our God (for example, creation, Noah's flood, the great escape from Egypt, and the teaching of the prophets), and God's law, the ten commandments given through Moses to the people to help them live well and in line with God's will. Although these are old, ancient things, they are precious to us because they help us get to know God and live as his friends. We don't just throw them out because Jesus has come. Jesus valued them himself, and told his followers to go on valuing them.

Now introduce the new thing, explaining why it is treasured, important and valuable. In our faith there are also new things which we as Christians value and treasure. With the coming of Jesus, we are able to have a completely new kind of friendship with God that had never before been possible. Through Jesus dying, rising and returning to heaven, we are able to have the gift of God's life breathed into our own lives. That means that every new morning of our lives there are new possibilities in our daily friendship with the living God!

Not only are we looking forward to the coming of God's kingdom at the end of all time – we can also enjoy living in it now. In Matthew 13:31-33, 44-52 Jesus gave us some ideas of what the kingdom of God is like. Here is just one of them.

It's like some treasure you might find in a field. (You could have an exciting-looking treasure box there.) You're so excited about this precious treasure that you go and sell everything else you have, just so you can buy the field and own the treasure. Let's think about that. If you found a diamond ring, would you go and sell your house and car and World Cup coin collection to get hold of it? Probably not. You'd only bother to sell your house and car and cherished possessions if the treasure you had found was worth far, far more than all the things you already had. Jesus is saying that knowing God in a loving friendship and living in him each day is actually worth far, far more than anything else you own.

I don't think many of us realise that yet. It's as if we dig up a treasure box, look at it and think, 'Oh, that's interesting – a box of treasure. I'll pop over and look at it sometime.' Then we bury it again and go home to carry on living in the same old way without realising what we're missing out on. Next time you catch a glimpse of what God is really like, and how incredibly wonderful he really is, commit yourself to doing something about it, so you can enjoy that treasure of living in peace and love with him every day of the rest of your life.

Robes of righteousness

As people come into church make sure that everyone is given a small picture or cut-out paper shape of a robe of righteousness, with this title on it:

Probably we have sometimes looked into our wardrobes before a party and decided that we have nothing suitable to wear. However jam-packed the wardrobe is, with all that extra junk stuffed in to keep it out of sight, we can't find anything we want to wear! Prepare to be impressed: the wardrobe space of today's teaching is quite something.

Mention the piece of paper they were all given when they came in, checking for any who have been missed and providing for them now. Everyone has been given a beautiful wedding garment! That's what used to happen when guests were invited to palaces. It was the practice for kings to provide thousands of guests with a suitable robe each from their vast wardrobes in which thousands of garments were kept ready specially for such occasions. (Dress a volunteer up in a clean white robe – a surplice is fine.) They had special servants to be in charge of those huge wardrobes.

In Jesus' parable of the wedding feast (see Matthew 22:1-14) we can imagine all the poor and the dirty straggling along to the palace in their smelly rags, and the people in charge of the king's wardrobes fitting up everyone with a clean, beautiful robe to wear, before ushering them into the grand dining hall. No doubt they felt different dressed like this – perhaps they even walked taller and were more polite to each other than usual! Then the king comes in to inspect his guests. (Perhaps everyone sits up straighter, like you do when someone important walks into assembly.) He is glad to see the palace full of guests who have accepted his invitation, because the original guests had refused to come. Everything is light and warm and happy.

Suddenly the king finds a guest who has accepted his invitation but rudely refused to wear the proper clothes provided. He's still in the filthy rags he came in, and the king has him put outside in the darkness with those who had chosen to turn down his invitation.

What is Jesus teaching us in this parable? One thing is that God is very happy to invite all of us to the Church of Christ and feed us here with love and rejoicing. So we can be happy together in God's company and enjoy ourselves in our worship. The other thing is that if we say yes to God, we do need to let him reclothe us, and not expect to go on wearing the rags of bickering and fighting, lying and cheating, self-indulgence and lack of self-control which we came in. That's why we always start our worship by saying sorry to God, and hearing his forgiveness, letting him clothe us with robes of righteousness.

Cancelling debts

First ask anyone who has never done anything wrong, *ever*, to raise their hand. Make it quite clear that doing wrong doesn't stop when you grow up, and it's a problem that we all have to deal with. In which case there's going to be another problem we need to deal with. What about when people do things wrong which hurt and upset us? It's bound to happen, and today we are given some very useful teaching from our Lord Jesus to help us with it.

Suppose someone lets you down, cheats on you, loses their temper with you and says some cruel unkind things, lets you down again, steals from you, makes you look stupid, and breaks something you've let them borrow. (Count on your fingers seven typical offences.) Peter goes to Jesus and says, 'Is seven times about the limit for forgiving someone? It seems fairly generous to me. You might as well give up on them after that, don't you agree? Or am I being a bit over-generous – more forgiving than is good for me?'

Jesus says, 'Actually, seven times isn't nearly enough! You need to keep on forgiving until you've lost count and just do it anyway.' And then he tells one of his stories to explain what he means (see Matthew 18:21-35).

Give a volunteer a sign to hold which says 'IOU millions'. The story is about a servant who owes loads and loads of money. He has a wife and children, and he's borrowed so much and has been using his plastic money facility so much that he's stacked up a huge debt to his master, which he can't pay off. The master calls for him (use another volunteer and give him a mobile phone or a smart jacket) and demands the money. The servant kneels down and begs (he does this) to be given more time to pay. The master feels sorry for the servant and lets him off the whole debt! Just like that! (Master draws a thick black line through the IOU.) How do you think the servant feels? (Collect ideas.)

Now that is what God has done for each of us. Ask them to think of all the things they've done wrong, perhaps which no one else knows about except them and God. Think of all the meanness, selfishness, pride, hypocrisy and so on that we have been forgiven completely by God. It's just as if we owed God millions of pounds (hold up the IOU) and God has drawn that line through it, setting us free from the debt.

So here is this happy, free servant, who finds a fellow servant owes him a few pounds. (Give another volunteer a sign with 'IOU a few pounds' on it.) And the same thing happens. The servant goes on his knees and begs (he does this) to be allowed more time to pay. But what does the servant do? He grabs him by the neck and shakes him (not too realistically) and has him thrown into prison until he pays up. What Jesus wants us to ask ourselves is this: Is it fair or right for the servant to behave like this? What do we think?

Next time we are not wanting to forgive someone, let's remember how God has treated us, and pass on that loving forgiveness time and time and time again.

Using God's gift

Beforehand place three boxes of different colours around the church. In the red box put five one-pound coins (cardboard ones are fine!), in the blue box put two one-pound coins and leave the yellow box empty.

We know that one day the world as we know it will come to an end. We know that life as we know it will finish. All the prophets and Jesus teach us in the Bible that there is going to be a Day of the Lord, when we will see Jesus in all God's glory, and all that is evil will not survive. That includes people. How we live now in our lives will affect what happens to us that day. We do need to know that.

When will it happen? We don't know the time or date; in fact, what we do know is that it will happen suddenly, without us having loads of time to change. That's why we need to live every day as if it were our last.

But God doesn't want us so scared of the last day that we can't enjoy life here. Jesus came to set us free from that fear, and, if we are walking through life as Jesus' friends, there is nothing to be frightened of, because it's only the evil and bad and selfish that will be destroyed; everything that is good and loving and honest will be gathered up safely for ever.

Jesus told one of his stories with secrets – parables – about making the most of all the gifts God has given us (see Matthew 25:14-30), and we need three people to help us with it. (Make sure that the third servant chosen has been warned beforehand that she will be told off in the story, and is confident enough to cope with that.)

In Jesus' story, a man is going on a long journey and, before he goes, he gathers his servants together and entrusts his property to them to look after. (Give five coins to one servant and send her off to find the red box. Give two coins to another servant and send him off to find the blue box. Give one coin to the last servant, and send her off to find the yellow box.) The man went off on his travels, and after a long time came back home. He called the servants to him to settle accounts with them. (Call the volunteers together with the boxes.) Let's see how the first servant has got on. (She opens the box and counts out to the owner ten coins. Be very pleased. Everyone can clap.) What about the second servant? (He opens the box and counts out four coins. Praise and applause.) What about the third servant? Tell everyone how this servant told the owner she was too scared to do anything with her gift, so she just hid it as it was. (She gives it back.) The owner was not pleased at all because the servant had not made good use of the gift she had been given. (Tell the servant off, and thank all the actors for their help.)

We all have gifts God has enjoyed giving us. Some of us are good at being friendly and welcoming, some good at looking after animals, working out money, ironing, or thinking out solutions to difficult problems. Whatever our gift is, we need to enjoy using it and making the most of it for the good of everyone.

Check your oil

Beforehand prepare some sticks with red paper flames stuck on the end.

Begin by asking who has ever been a bridesmaid or a page-boy at a wedding. Were any of them late for the wedding? Jesus once told a parable about some bridesmaids (see Matthew 25:1-13). Some were ready when they were needed, but some weren't.

Show the 'torches' which were used at that time. Material was soaked in oil and tied on to the end of sticks. When you set light to them they would burn well, so the bride and bridegroom, coming from the bridegroom's house in the evening of the wedding, could have their way lit by the bridesmaids' torches. (Have a bride and groom and some bridesmaids to show this, holding their torch sticks.) At least, they could if the bridesmaids had their oil with them.

The problem in Jesus' story was that half the bridesmaids hadn't checked their oil supplies, so when the bridegroom needed their torchlight, they were rushing off to buy more oil, and ended up being shut out of the wedding feast.

What is the hidden message in this parable? What is Jesus wanting us to understand?

He wants us to be ready, and have our oil supplies topped up, so that whenever the bridegroom returns, even if he takes longer to arrive than we were expecting, we will be there waiting, shining brightly in the darkness. Then the bridegroom can lead us all into the celebrations and the feast.

Fill the oil lamp and light it. God's Spirit is like the oil we need to keep us burning brightly with God's love. If we stop keeping ourselves 'topped up' by forgetting to pray and read the Bible each day, our lives will stop shining, just as the girls' torches went out. Then, if Jesus suddenly returns, unexpectedly, either at the end of time or in a situation where our bright Christian love is badly needed, we won't be able to help.

So Jesus is telling us to keep praying, keep listening and keep loving. That way, we'll be all ready whenever he needs us.

MIRACLES

Straightened up

Bring along a couple of long scarves tied together.

Ask a volunteer to help you explain today's teaching, and get them to stand on the scarf. Wind the scarf round the back of their neck, and join the two ends so that the volunteer is forced to stand bent forward, looking down in a fixed position. Looking sideways is quite difficult, and looking up and into people's faces is almost impossible. Remind everyone of the crippled woman in Luke 13:10-17, whose back was set into this position so that she had lived the last eighteen years of her life looking down at her feet, unable to see the world properly, or have a face-to-face conversation.

What Jesus did was to release her from this locked position. When he saw her he felt so sorry for her and longed to set her free. And when he placed his healing hands on her back and told her she could now move again (untie the scarf), she found that she could stand upright, and see all around and look into people's faces again! That felt wonderful, and she praised God for all she was worth.

Now ask for another volunteer, and tie them up in the same way. Explain how people can be just as crippled and stuck in their thinking and living, even though their bodies look and work quite normally. Habits of grumbling about everything, wishing for things we can't have, or being so set in our ways that when God asks us to help someone we see it as impossible because it doesn't fit in with our plans – these things can mean that spiritually we are stuck and unable to look up and around. So can spending all our time thinking of one thing, whether that is a hobby, an addiction, an ambition, our health or fitness, or even a person. If we haven't looked up to God's face for ages, we might find we're stuck in the 'head down' position.

God is offering to release us from such crippling habits. He is the one who can put his healing hands on our lives (untie the scarves) and set us free again. It feels so good, and no one needs to stay trapped any longer.

The ten lepers

Ask for ten volunteers and dish out 'bandages' for them to wear on arms, legs and head. Explain that they are lepers and, because the disease is thought to be very catching, they can't stay with everyone else here but must go and sit somewhere else. Direct them to a place separate from the rest of the congregation. As they go, tell everyone how the lepers of Jesus' day had to leave their homes and live right away from the villages and towns, and look after themselves. How must they have felt? Lonely? Left out? Guilty? Unacceptable? Frightened?

We may not have the disease of leprosy, but there are lots of people in our world, in our country and in our town – perhaps even in our church – who feel lonely, left out, guilty, unacceptable and frightened, like the lepers. People cry themselves to sleep and wake up feeling sad about the day ahead. People who have lost contact with friends, or whose loved ones have died, try hard to be cheerful when they have a big ache of sadness inside them. Lots of people are hurting, and longing for their life to be different.

That's how these ten lepers felt that morning when they saw Jesus walking along the road on his way to a village (see Luke 17:11-19). They couldn't come too close to him, but they came as close as they could, and shouted to him, 'Jesus, Master, have pity on us!' (This can be written on a sign so the ten 'lepers' can shout it out.) People still cry out to God in their hearts like this. Does God hear?

He certainly does! Jesus shows us what God is like, and what Jesus did was to tell the lepers to go and show themselves to the priest. Whyever did he tell them that? Because if you were a leper and you were healed, you had to show yourself to a priest, so he could check you over and pronounce you fit and well.

Send your lepers off to the priest, who has ten cards saying, 'I declare this leper is now CLEAN. Signed: Revd. John Hayward.' Tell them that when they have their certificate of health they are free to join the other people in the congregation.

If any of the volunteers decides to come and say 'thank you' you can of course use this and praise it. However, since they haven't actually been healed of anything, they will probably all sit down in their places. Tell everyone how one leper (choose one) came back to Jesus to say 'thank you'. All the others had been keen to talk to Jesus when they needed something, but they forgot him once he had sorted them out.

Let's make sure that when God answers our prayers, we don't forget to say thank you – even if his answer is not the answer we expect.

Lazarus

You will need an inflatable ball or a balloon, and, if possible, a dummy used for teaching mouth-to-mouth resuscitation. Otherwise, bring along a large baby doll.

Begin by asking everyone to breathe in deeply, hold their breath while you count to twenty and then let their breath out. They will all have noticed how much we need that air. By the end of just twenty seconds we're getting desperate! Most of the time we breathe in and out without even thinking about it. Although it's such a vitally important thing to do, we're designed so that the breathing mostly goes on automatically so we can do lots of other things at the same time. Yet without that breathing we wouldn't be able to do any of those other things because we would be dead. That's how important breath is – it's a matter of life and death.

Ask a volunteer to demonstrate what we have to do if we come across someone whose breathing has stopped. Point out that what is happening when we are doing mouth-to-mouth resuscitation is that we actually do the breathing for the other person. With our living breath we can save someone's life.

In John 11:1-44 there is an amazing story of Jesus actually bringing someone back to life. It was his friend Lazarus, and when Jesus' voice, as the Lord of life, broke into the place of death, Lazarus heard his name being called and walked out into life again towards that voice.

Jesus calls each of us by name. He calls into the place we are, even if that place is full of darkness and sadness, or if the noise of unimportant things we like wasting our time on nearly drowns his voice, or if we're running as fast as we can away from God's way of living. Wherever we are, Jesus keeps calling because he wants to bring us out into new life. He knows his breath in us will transform our time in this life, and beyond that into the time after our physical death. As Jesus breathes his life into us it will make such a difference to us that we'll wish we'd gone for it ages ago!

Ask someone to blow up the ball or balloon, and as they do so point out what a difference it is making to have that breath inside. Once they are filled with our breath they have a whole new dimension – they're much more useful and they're much more their true selves. It's the same with us. When we let God breathe his life into us every minute of every day, we become much more our true selves, our life has a whole new dimension, and we are of more use to God in caring for the world he loves.

Jesus feeds the people

Begin by asking people how they like to spend their pocket money. Invite representatives of all ages to join in this. Has anyone ever spent their money on something which has let them down, or been disappointing, so that they end up wishing they had saved their money? Ask a few people to share their experiences.

It may be that you have had to watch as someone you are fond of wastes their money. You can see that it's all going to end in disappointment, or even tragedy, but they won't listen to you, and all you can do is stand by and wait to pick up the pieces when it all goes wrong, without saying, 'I told you so'! It's our love for the other person that makes us ache to see them wasting their money like that; because we love them we want better for them than to be sad and disappointed by things that aren't worth buying.

That's how it is with our parent God, who loves us to bits, and aches as he watches as we spend not just our money but our time and our love on things which are not going to be good for us, or satisfying or rewarding. He wants better for us than that. God wants us to be aware of our need for his love and power in our lives, and to come to him for it, because he is happy to give it to us free.

Look at all those people in Matthew 14:13-21. Why had they bothered to leave their towns and villages and walk miles out into the country? They bothered because they knew their need of Jesus and were prepared to 'spend' their whole day looking for him and listening to him, hanging on his words. What did Jesus do? Did he let them down or disappoint them? No! He was there for them, ready to heal the sick friends and relations they had brought, ready to reassure them that God loved them, and teach them about how they could best please God in their lives.

And when their tummies started rumbling, and they knew physical hunger as well as spiritual hunger, what did Jesus do? He fed them! All he used was what they had. That's what he always uses. Are you a three- or four-year-old, ready for Jesus to use your life? Then that's what he'll use to make lots of other people really happy. Are you a seventy- or eighty-year-old, ready for Jesus to use your life? Then that's what he'll use to bring blessing and hope to lots of other people. And it's the same with all the rest of us in between.

What about our church? Is St Martin's ready to be used by Jesus? If we are, he will use us, and lots of people in this area will be blessed and given hope; if we aren't, and can't be bothered to go and spend time seeking Jesus out and listening to him, then he won't be using us and the people in our area will lose out.

Let's make sure that doesn't happen. Our job is to make ourselves available, and help give out to the people the gifts of God, so that all are properly fed.

Walking on water

If you know a juggler, invite them to come and juggle as part of today's talk. Failing this, give out some balloons to a group of older children and ask them to keep them in the air, in as controlled a way as possible, using hands, head, knees and feet.

As the juggler or children perform, draw attention to the way they need to concentrate and keep their eyes on the balls or balloons if they are to be sure of catching them under control. Notice how the moment they lose concentration, or lose balance, things go wrong.

In Matthew 14:22-33 we hear about some people in a boat, weathering a terrible storm. It was the disciples, and Jesus had sent them off home while he himself went off to pray on his own after he had fed all those five thousand people. He needed to be alone with his heavenly Father to talk that over, and give special thanks for all that had happened. The waves were churning, and the boat was rocking and the disciples were frightened – especially when they saw Jesus walking across to them. This was water, and you can't walk on that! We are told they thought Jesus must be a ghost, and they got more scared than ever.

Let's look at what Peter did next. He called out to Jesus, 'If it really is you, then tell me to come to you over the water.' Why did he say that? What was he doing? It sounds as if he was testing whether Jesus was real or not, like us saying to a friend, 'If you've really been up in space, show me a photograph to prove it', or 'If you really love me, how about helping with this washing-up'.

Jesus knows he isn't a ghost, and he takes Peter up on what he's asked. 'Come on, then!' he says. There's no way out now! Peter concentrates on Jesus, like the juggler concentrated on the balls. He gets as far as climbing out of the boat, and he starts to walk towards Jesus, still concentrating on him, and then suddenly it all hits him. 'This is crazy! This is impossible! The water can't possibly be holding my weight! Rationally I know I ought to be sinking!' And as those doubts make him panic and lose his sight of Jesus, he does just that – he starts to sink and has to shout out in terror to Jesus to save him. And, of course, Jesus reaches out to him and gets him to safety straightaway.

Trusting Jesus is keeping ourselves concentrating on him and his love, underneath everything else that we do. Suppose you're buying some sweets. At the same time you're aware of Jesus and his love. What difference does that make? You will probably buy without being greedy, and you'll probably end up sharing what you get. Suppose you are travelling to work, and you've also got your eyes on Jesus. That will affect the way you drive, and the way you treat other commuters.

Today Jesus is saying to each of us, 'Yes, it is OK for you to put your total trust in me. Just keep that in mind and all the things which make you feel frightened and insecure will not let you sink – you can walk straight over them, confident in my love and power.'

SPECIAL DAYS

Christmas Day

Bring something with you to offer as a small gift – a chocolate bar, a sticker, a few flowers or a piece of fruit, perhaps.

Over Christmas we have all been busy giving one another presents. Explain that you have brought something with you to give away today, so that we can understand a bit more about God's Christmas present to us. In Jesus we see God giving himself to set us free from sin and evil because he loves us so much.

Show everyone what your gift is, and ask them to put their hands up if they would like to be considered for it. Choose someone using some random method, such as their name being first in the alphabet, or their birthday coming up this week. When God gives us his present no one has to get left out. Everyone who asks, gets.

Stand a short distance away from the person chosen, and hold out the gift. Can they receive the gift without moving? No, they can't. If we are going to receive a gift we have to change our position a bit. (The person can demonstrate this and receive the gift.) It's the same with us all receiving God's gift – we are bound to change if we receive Jesus into our daily living.

Just as Joseph and Mary's lives changed when Jesus was born into their family, so our lives will change. As we reach out to receive Jesus, we shall find we are able to reach out to one another in a more loving, positive way; we shall find we are more concerned about justice and mercy being written into our social system; we shall find we are wanting to be more truthful to others and ourselves.

So be prepared – if you don't want to change into a happier, more loving person, freed from guilt and able to be truly yourself, then don't take God up on his offer!

Epiphany

Beforehand arrange for a knitter to bring a completed garment to church, together with a ball of wool and needles. Also prepare a large paper cut-out of a similar garment, which is folded up so that the first bit that would be made is the only piece showing. Alternatively use the actual garment, folded up at that point.

Begin by showing everyone the wonderful garment that the knitter has made and asking how long it took to make and who it is for. What did it look like at first, when they started making it? The knitter can show the ball of wool and needles, and do a couple of stitches. Hold up the needles with these stitches and point out that it doesn't look much like a jumper/ scarf yet! But the knitter went on working at it, knowing that one day it would be ready.

God knew that one day everything would be ready for Jesus to come into the world, but he, too, took a long time making things ready. He started by calling one person, Abraham. (Show the folded garment, but don't refer to it – it is there to be visual reinforcement of what you are saying.) Over the years God went on to prepare all Abraham's family. (More of the garment is revealed.) Until over more years that family became one nation. (Reveal some more of the garment.) But God's plan still wasn't finished. He went on to include not one nation but all the nations and everyone in them. (Shake the whole garment out and display it.) Today is called the Epiphany because the word 'epiphany' means 'showing' or 'revealing' or 'manifesting', and when those wise men arrived at Bethlehem with their presents, God was showing or revealing himself not just to Abraham or his family, not just to the whole nation of Israel, but to all the rest of us in the world as well.

Whatever country you come from, whatever you look like and whatever language you speak, God is saying to us today that he is there for you and no one is left out. You don't have to have the right ancestors to know God. You don't have to pass any exams to know God.

We sometimes get so interested in the presents the wise men were bringing to Jesus that we forget what brought them there in the first place. It was God who called these wise men from other nations to be there when Jesus was still a baby, so he could welcome them as well. They were there representing all the nations, so when God welcomed them he was welcoming each of us.

Mothering Sunday

Begin by interviewing a couple of mothers, one young and one older, using such questions as: What do you like best about being a mum? What do you find hardest? How has being a mum helped you grow as a person? What advice would you give to a young Christian couple about to become parents?

Talk about the way we all need to look after each other in this unselfish, loving way which we think of as mothering, and how that is the way our loving God treats us. He doesn't smother us or stop us exploring our world and trying everything out, but he encourages us and guides us so we know where to walk safely. If we fall over and hurt ourselves in life, he's there to comfort us and make us better, and if we go off and get ourselves lost in bad or stupid behaviour, he comes to search for us until he finds us, calling our name again and again until we hear him and shout out, asking to be rescued.

When we are little, our parents have to dress us, because we can't do our buttons up or tie our laces on our own. A good way to remember that we are all called to look after one another in a loving, caring way, is to think about it as dressing ourselves in clothes of kindness, forgiveness and patience, compassion, humility and gentleness. As you say this, dress a volunteer or a rag doll in various garments. Finally, to bind everything together, we need love (a belt is tied around the other clothes).

So tomorrow, and every morning when you get dressed, think of yourself also putting on the clothes of kindness, forgiveness and patience, compassion, humility and gentleness, and tie everything together with love (see Colossians 3:12-14). That way we'll be learning to look after one another the way our God looks after us.

Palm Sunday

Ask about football matches people have watched which have been really memorable and exciting. If you happen to have any players in the congregation, ask them to talk about a particularly memorable moment of triumph, and how it felt to have the spectators sharing the exhilaration.

When Jesus rode into Jerusalem all the crowds were on his side, cheering, waving and singing, pushing for the best view, and excited not just with Jesus as a hero but at what was a turning point for their side – their country. There would have been some there on that first Palm Sunday who saw it as a political statement, others as religious revival, others as a festive carnival of some kind.

So why did Jesus ride into Jerusalem on a donkey?

He was doing something the scriptures had said would happen to the promised Messiah. This meant he was giving a very strong hint to the people about who he was. He was saying that the Messiah had now come and was entering the holy city of Jerusalem as a king. But instead of all the rich clothes and grandeur of an earthly king, Jesus was riding on a very humble animal that was often piled high with people's luggage and shopping. It was a bit like using a shopper bike rather than a Rolls Royce, stretched limo or BMW.

All the crowds that day cheered Jesus, but a few days later, once he didn't look like a winner any more, many of the same people had turned against him and were yelling for his blood.

What kind of supporters are we? Do we support our team only when it's doing really well, or do we hang in there even after a run of lost games? Do we stick with our friends even when they go through a bad patch? Do we keep trying even when a marriage gets shaky? And, perhaps most important of all, are we happy to sing God's praise in church on Sunday but ignore him or deny him by our behaviour and language and choices during the week?

These are Palm Sunday questions which we need to ask ourselves today.

Good Friday

Have the London underground map printed out on the weekly sheet, or have some larger versions available to show everyone.

Look at the plan and talk about the way it is simple sign language to help us make sense of a huge complicated network of rails and tunnels criss-crossing under the streets. The whole thing is so enormous to understand that we need this simple map.

But when we travel on the underground it only works because, as well as the simple map in our hand or on the station wall, the real massive tracks are laid in all those dark tunnels, and the electrical power is surging through all the thick cables, and the tilers have been busy fixing tiles on the station walls, and the computers are busy checking where each train is so that they don't bump into one another, and those moving stairs, the escalators, are well oiled and running smoothly. Although all this doesn't show up on our plan of coloured lines and blobs, we only have to look at it and we know that all the real stuff is right there.

In a way the cross shape is like one of those plans. Draw people's attention to the crosses they can see around them in church. It is only a simple shape, and we can all make it ourselves by placing one index finger across the other. (Do that now.) When people say 'fingers crossed' what do they do? (Ask some people to show this.) Today it usually means hoping we'll be lucky, but a long time ago it was people making the sign of the cross as they prayed about something they were worried about. (We could go back to using the sign that way!)

Now if the shape of the cross is like the underground train plan, what is all the real, deep stuff that the cross reminds us of? Ask everyone to find or make a cross and look at it, as you tell them about the deeper meaning: God loves the world so much that he was willing to give up everything, and come and live with us in person as Jesus. That loving led him to a cross where he gave up his life for us, taking all the selfishness and sin on himself, and stretching out his arms in welcome and forgiveness, because he so longs for us to be free.

Easter Sunday

Bring along a few fresh eggs in a carton, and a chocolate egg.

Begin by reminding everyone that we are here for an exciting celebration. Draw attention to all the flowers, and the cleaning that has been going on, and any banners or other special Easter decorations and symbols. What is it we're celebrating? That Jesus had died on the cross and is now alive – alive for ever!

Introduce the chocolate egg. For some reason we've been seeing a lot of these at Easter. No doubt some people gave some away. No doubt some ate one before breakfast! What have they got to do with Jesus? Why do we all like to give one another eggs at Easter time?

One reason is that people were giving one another eggs around the time of Easter long before they had heard about Jesus. This is springtime, and eggs are all part of the spring, with its promise of new life.

New life! That's interesting – we've been hearing about the new life that Jesus gives us. When people came to our country and told us about Jesus, they thought the egg was a very good way of explaining the Gospel, so they kept it.

How does an egg help us to understand the Easter story? Show everyone the carton of ordinary eggs, and hold one up on its own. What is it? (An egg.) What comes out of a fertilised egg like this? (A chicken.) Yes, it's a new life – in this case a chicken. An egg is the way new creatures come into being. And Easter is about Jesus being alive in a new way and making it possible for all of us to be given new life.

What does the inside of an egg look like? (It's got yellow yolk and some thick runny stuff which is white when it's cooked.) What are some favourite ways of eating an egg? (Gather suggestions.) So what is inside the shell turns into something quite different. Jesus' life now, as from the first Easter Day, is different. For a start, he's never going to die again; his new life isn't a life that runs out. Even though Jesus has now been alive again for nearly two thousand years, he is outside time, so he hasn't got old. And he isn't tied to space like us, so he can come and go without having to catch a bus or open doors. He doesn't have to be seen to be real.

Now break one of the eggs. When we enjoy eating an egg

the shell needs to be broken; otherwise we wouldn't be able to get at the white and the yolk. When a chick is ready to live in the big wide world it has to crack the eggshell before it can climb out. What does that tell us? Sometimes we want to hang on to things just as they are. We don't always want to change, even if change in our lives is for the best.

Will we let our shells be broken ready for the new life Jesus wants us to have? God is calling us out of our shells into a whole new, different way of living. It is the loving way of living, trusting in God with our heart and soul and mind and strength, and loving one another. That may mean that some of our habits and fears may, like shells, have to be broken before we can live freely in the loving way. The good news of Easter is that Jesus has already broken through death and sin, so if we hold on to him, he can bring us through the shell breaking and out into the light and space of day – a daylight which lasts for ever.

Ascension Day

Begin by staging a Mexican wave, which runs through the whole church or assembly. Point out how it only worked so well because all of us as individuals were working together as a unit of energy.

Remind everyone of the events leading up to today, giving them a whistle-stop tour of Jesus' life, death, Resurrection and post-Resurrection appearances. Explain how the disciples needed that time to get used to Jesus being alive and around, though not always visible or physically present.

Now they were ready for the next stage in the plan. Jesus leads them out of the city and he gives them his blessing, telling them to hang around Jerusalem without rushing off to do their own bit of mission work. (Enthusiasm is wonderful but it can sometimes make us race off to start before we've got everything we need.) The disciples have got to wait because God is going to send the Holy Spirit to empower them and equip them for the work they will be doing. It will make it possible for the news of God's love to spread out through the world like our Mexican wave.

When Jesus had finished giving the disciples their instructions and his encouragement, we are told that the disciples watched him being taken into heaven, until a cloud hid him from their sight. Those are the only practical details we have, so we don't know exactly how it happened. But we do know that the disciples were in no doubt about where Jesus had gone, and they were full of joy and excitement as they made their way back to the city to wait for the Holy Spirit, as Jesus had told them to.

A lot of years have gone by since Jesus ascended into heaven – nearly two thousand years. But that isn't much if you aren't stuck in time as we are, and God isn't stuck in time. He's prepared to wait to give us humans the chance to turn to him in our lives, and we don't know the date when Jesus will return. We do know that in God's good time he will come back, and everyone will see his glory together, both the living and those who have finished the earthly part of their life.

In the meantime, we have been given the Holy Spirit, so that God can be with us in person every moment of our life, helping us and guiding our choices, steering us safely through temptations, and teaching us more and more about our amazing God. All he waits for is to be invited.

Pentecost

Bring along an electrical appliance and, if necessary, an extension lead. Alternatively, have a torch or game powered by batteries, and keep the batteries separate at first.

Refresh everyone's memory of today's dynamic event, with the disciples praying and waiting on God, and the early morning experience of his power coming to them like a rushing wind, or flames, searching out each one of them and touching them with the touch of God.

It quite overwhelmed them, and left them fired up with excitement at what God is capable of doing in people. They were bursting to tell everyone else about it, and wanted everyone to share this sense of God actually living in them. It was quite different from knowing about God; it was even different from walking about in the company of Jesus. This was like being flowed through with new life that set them living, talking and working in a new way.

Show the electrical appliance you have brought. Explain what this thing is capable of doing, but point out that at the moment it can't do any of those things. It has everything in place to work in that lively way, but something is missing at the moment – it isn't linked up to the power supply. Would it help if the appliance knew exactly how electricity works? Not really. However much is known about electrical circuits and the power grid, that won't bring this appliance to life. What it needs is this. (Plug the appliance into the power supply and switch on.)

Now the thing springs into life, and all kinds of potential are activated. That's what it's like having God's Spirit living in us and flowing through us. It makes that much difference! Just think what our world could be like if we were all full of the power of God's Spirit. Just think what a difference it would make in the world if all those in churches today all over the world asked God, seriously and openly, for a fresh outpouring of the Holy Spirit!

So often we are like well-finished appliances or games, knowing all about God's power, but not wanting to have the power switched on in us, just in case. Just in case what? Our God is the true, living God of love and compassion and mercy.

Which means that any power he sends to touch us and affect us, will be only and entirely good for us. God is longing for his Church to be 'live' with the active power of his Spirit; we may be in good working order, but we also need to have the power, so that we actually 'work'!

Trinity Sunday

Beforehand prepare a cake. Also get together two eggs, a bag of sugar, a bag of flour and some margarine, and a mixing bowl, cake tin and wooden spoon.

Set the cake tin down and tell everyone that today we are going to have a cake again, because it is Trinity Sunday. So we are going to have a Trinity cake. Ask various helpers to bring the eggs, sugar and flour and margarine and place them in the cake tin.

Proudly present the cake, inviting everyone to take a slice, and let the children point out to you that you haven't got a cake at all. You've just got the ingredients. But isn't a cake just ingredients, then? Let them help you understand that you'd have to mix them together and cook them before you had a cake.

Now let it suddenly dawn on you that it's a bit like that with the nature of God. God is the Father who created the world, Jesus Christ who saved us, and the Holy Spirit who gives life to the people of God. But they aren't separate from each other, any more than these separate ingredients are a cake. To be a cake all the ingredients need to be co-operating and working together. Then they become something which is not eggs, flour, sugar and margarine. Produce the real cake and point out that you wouldn't say, 'Have a slice of eggs, flour, margarine and sugar with your cup of tea.' You'd call it by its name: a cake.

In the same kind of way, when we talk about God we are talking about our Maker, and we're talking about the risen Jesus who has rescued us from sin and death, and we're talking about the Holy Spirit who brings us into new life. We know that the word 'God' means all three persons in a wonderful harmony, a community which is still One.

Give the Trinity cake to whoever is in charge of refreshments after the service, so it can be shared out then.

Thematic Index

Biblical Reference Index